Journey toward Maximum Faith

Your Personal Workbook

Terry Carlsor
Mike Calacci

FEATURING INTRODUCTION, RESEARCH,
WORLDVIEW MATERIALS, AND FOREWORD BY

Dr. George Barna

FOR USE WITH

Arizona Christian University Worldview Assessment and
Maximum Faith: Live Like Jesus, Experience Genuine Transformation
by Dr. George Barna

ARIZONA CHRISTIAN UNIVERSITY PRESS

JOURNEY TOWARD MAXIMUM FAITH

Your Personal Workbook

A collaborative project by Terry Carlson & Mike Calacci (Journey Coaching) and Dr. George Barna (Cultural Research Center at Arizona Christian University).

For use with the Arizona Christian University Worldview Assessment and *Maximum Faith: Live Like Jesus, Experience Genuine Transformation* by Dr. George Barna (2011).

Cover art and interior design by MN Design

Arizona Christian University Press is the book-publishing division of Arizona Christian University, a private Christian university in Glendale, Arizona, that provides a biblically integrated, liberal arts education equipping graduates to serve the Lord Jesus Christ in all aspects of life, as leaders of influence and excellence. Arizona Christian University exists to educate and equip followers of Christ to transform culture with truth.

Requests for permissions should be addressed to:
Arizona Christian University Press
1 W. Firestorm Way
Glendale, AZ 85306

ISBN: 979-8-9899581-0-8

Printed in the United States of America

More information about Journey Coaching is available at: **JourneyCoaching.org**. More information about the Cultural Research Center at Arizona Christian University is available at **CulturalResearchCenter.com**. More information about the Arizona Christian University Worldview Assessment is available at: **ACUworldview.com**

DISCLAIMER OF LIABILITY

Neither the authors, nor the Cultural Research Center at Arizona Christian University, make any warranty with respect to the content of this book. The parties expressly disclaim any and all liability for any damage, loss, or liability caused by or alleged to be caused by the content of this book, any recommendation included in this book, or any error in or omission of content from this book, whether arising from the parties' intentional action, negligence, or otherwise.

No content provided in this book is intended as a medical diagnosis or medical advice of any kind. All content in this book is provided based on the authors' personal experiences and opinions only, and is not intended as a substitute for the advice of licensed medical personnel. The reader should regularly consult licensed medical personnel with respect to any issues that may suggest a medical condition, whether mental or physical.

CONTENTS

FOREWORD
DR. GEORGE BARNA

One of the biggest challenges facing people of faith today is how difficult it is to navigate the culture and consistently live out God's truth in their lives—actually thinking and living as Jesus would have us do. Cultural headwinds seem to push us further and further from what we know to be true, further from what God desires for each of us—and further from what our hearts longed for when we first came to know Jesus. And we increasingly feel we are alone in our journey to walk more closely with God.

My research bears this out. It's harder than ever to practice authentic, biblical faith.

A number of years ago I wrote a book called *Maximum Faith: Live Like Jesus, Experience Genuine Transformation* (2011). Based on a massive study of more than 17,000 people's faith experience, it offers a spiritual roadmap, identifying 10 stops on the journey to spiritual wholeness.

That research emphasized that most Christians become stuck after getting "saved"—they become Christians, but never experience the deeper, genuine transformation that leads them to consistently think and live like Jesus. Salvation (acknowledging our sinfulness, agreeing to repent, and asking Jesus to save us and lead us forward), is only the fourth stop of 10 on the journey! In fact, most Christians stop well short of reaching what I call "maximum faith." Sadly, most Christians will never experience the life God desires for them.

And today, a substantial number of adults—two out of three—self-identify as Christians, but only 4% of them actually have a biblical worldview![1] In other words, the overwhelming majority of Christians never learn to think and act like Jesus.

We're still getting stuck!

That's why I'm so excited about collaborating with the Journey team on this new worldview resource, *Journey toward Maximum Faith*.

It brings together key principles from four decades of worldview research (including those outlined in *Maximum Faith*) and combines it with my latest practical tool, the Arizona Christian University Worldview Assessment, a new online assessment that provides a detailed picture of an individual's worldview. And *Journey toward Maximum Faith* puts both of these essential worldview elements in the context of what the Journey team does best—one-on-one coaching.

In my decades of research, I've come to understand that one of the most powerful tools to overcome the prevailing worldview drift and to get "unstuck" in life is the simple principle of not being alone on the journey.

Specifically, my research shows that having someone to walk with as a coach or mentor—offering wisdom, accountability, and encouragement—is one of the surest ways for a believer to deepen and refine their understanding and application of God's truth.

It's the path of discipleship—learning from someone else who is further along the road than you are. Walking through life with them in a relationship of trust. Having someone to talk through questions and wrestle with how best to apply God's truth. Interacting with a person you trust to hear your doubts and frustrations. And to have another person share in the victories when you overcome old patterns and see God and His truth operating more fully in your life.

This was the essence of Jesus' ministry—calling His disciples to be in relationship with Him, to hear His teachings, and to try (and sometimes fail) to consistently apply His truths to their lives. That's how His followers learned to become genuine disciples.

Jesus offered the example of the personal coaching relationship as the primary context for shaping this ragtag bunch of (often very deficient) followers into effective agents of transformation. It's a model that we can still use today to become disciples of Jesus in our own lives and to help others become disciples—and to live a life of "maximum faith."

Discipleship is the goal of our faith—and coaching is how Jesus facilitated that outcome. We see this principle in play throughout His ministry. He built a trust-based relationship with the apostles. He invested time in reading and discussing the Scriptures with them. He demonstrated what love and service looked look by living such a life among them. He gave them feedback on their choices and held them accountable for their behavior. In short, He was a model coach, giving His disciples first-hand experience in what great spiritual mentoring looks like.

That is what Jesus, in turn, calls us to do. As He commands in Matthew 28:19-20: "Therefore, go and make disciples of all nations, baptizing them in the name of the Father and of the Son and of the Holy Spirit, and teaching them to obey everything I have commanded you. And surely I am with you always, to the very end of the age."

What does the process of becoming a disciple look like? As I share in my recent book, *Raising Spiritual Champions: Nurturing Your Child's Heart, Mind and Soul*, discipleship involves four fundamental practices—all of which are best undertaken with another person.[2]

- Making a life-defining commitment to be a disciple of Jesus
- Accepting the biblical principles and commands that lead to becoming a disciple
- Adopting the lifestyle of a disciple—obedience through the applications of beliefs
- Inviting personal accountability and stability—through assessing what matters, reinforcing growth, and celebrating disciplehood[3]

The biblical worldview isn't rocket science; it is simply possessing a decision-making filter that compels you to think like Jesus so that you can act like Jesus. And the journey to develop this worldview is best done in relationship with a coach or mentor.

The Journey team gets this! And this resource will help you, too, to understand and embody that approach to discipleship.

At the Cultural Research Center at Arizona Christian University, we are excited about *Journey toward Maximum Faith*, a collaborative resource that brings together my decades of worldview research and the Journey team's coaching expertise.

My hope is that *Journey toward Maximum Faith*, used along with the Arizona Christian University Worldview Assessment, will help a new movement of God's people to get "unstuck"—and to be unwilling to settle for anything less than being fully devoted to God and becoming all that He wants His people to be.

Enjoy the Journey!

George Barna

Director of Research, Cultural Research Center at Arizona Christian University

Author, *Raising Spiritual Champions: Nurturing Your Child's Heart, Mind and Soul* (2023) and *Maximum Faith* (2011; reprint 2023).

Professor, Arizona Christian University

[1] George Barna, "Incidence of Biblical Worldview Shows Significant Change Since the Start of the Pandemic," Release #1, American Worldview Inventory 2023, Cultural Research Center at Arizona Christian University, February 28, 2023. Available at: https://www.arizonachristian.edu/wp-content/uploads/2023/02/CRC_AWVI2023_Release1.pdf

[2] George Barna, *Raising Spiritual Champions: Nurturing Your Child's Heart, Mind and Soul* (Arizona Christian University Press, 2023; with Fedd Books).

[3] George Barna, *Raising Spiritual Champions: Nurturing Your Child's Heart, Mind and Soul* (Arizona Christian University Press, 2023; with Fedd Books), 62.

Introduction

Imagine trying on a new set of glasses that allow you to see things with greater clarity and wonder than ever before. We hope this journey does that for you, that it sharpens your focus on everything in and around you. Welcome to a new adventure where you will have an opportunity to learn some exciting things about yourself, others, and about God. This adventure will take you on a journey to better understand how you see the world and open your eyes to more clearly see how our awesome and Holy God sees it. We expect this journey will be both encouraging and challenging, that it will provide a place to grow and better see yourself as a person made in the image of God.

On this journey you will celebrate God's past work in your life. You will also be given the opportunity to see and experience yourself and God in new ways, ways that allow you to grow to see the world the way God sees it. With this new perspective, the door will be open to life changes, changes that can lead to greater peace and joy as you see the world and live as God intended. This change will only come when you recognize the need to give up trying to live and act under your own authority. When you position yourself under the authority of God and trust His Word in your life, you can experience the endless filling of the power of God's Spirit. This is the only way we can find maximum freedom, maximum power, and maximum peace in our lives. This is the only way we can experience maximum faith. This series, *Journey toward Maximum Faith*, was designed to help you understand and identify ways to move toward this type of closer relationship with God and others.

If you have already gone through the first workbook, *Starting the Journey*, you are in an excellent place to build on the trust and understanding you have with your coach. This foundation will lead you to a deeper focus on worldview with an eye toward moving to maximum faith. It might be helpful to think about maximum faith as being or becoming as much like Christ as is possible in this life. In his book *Maximum Faith: Live Like Jesus, Experience Genuine Transformation*, author George Barna describes the transformation we all must all go through toward maximum faith. We must learn to love God and other people in four key dimensions of who He made us to be: heart, soul, mind, and strength. In this, Dr. Barna is borrowing Jesus' own words (Mark 12:30–31). It would also be helpful to think of maximum faith not as a destination, but as a journey where we continue to grow in a relationship with God through Jesus Christ and become more and more like Him until we leave this earth for eternal life.

Maybe you are excited about the possibility of learning to become more like Christ through this coaching series. Alternatively, perhaps you are feeling a little confused and discouraged: "I thought all I had to do was be good or say a prayer to get my ticket to Heaven? Now you are telling me I have to keep growing to know and become more like Jesus?" If that is how you are feeling, it is our hope that you will hang on with us as we explore what becoming like Christ means and how it can help you experience a fullness of life and joy that you likely never felt possible.

What to Expect

Journey is kind of like a self-help book but with a twist. The twist is that you will get so much more out of any growth process if you don't try to do it alone. Going on this journey with another person is more productive and fruitful than going it alone. That is why *Journey* is built on a simple and informal coaching model. If you don't already have a coach, consider asking a friend or family member to go through it with you. There are many ways to do this, but the ideal setting would be where you invite someone whose faith and life inspires you to grow. This could be someone who is a little older or more mature, specifically a person you would like to have speak into your life from their own experience. This person would be your coach. We also encourage you to pray together at the beginning of each session. Prayer helps us remember our dependence on God and enables us to call upon His Spirit to guide us toward healthy, fulfilling, and lasting growth.

It is important for you to keep your Bible handy as you study and share with each other. It can help you deepen your understanding of biblical worldview and begin to experience the love and relationship with God through His Word. Plus, it becomes the ultimate measuring rod for accuracy. We have worked very hard to make sure that

Journey resources are biblically sound, but don't just take our words (or others) for granted without comparing them to Scripture.

Worldview

In this *Journey* series we are going to talk a lot about the concept of worldview. We cannot grow to be more like Christ until we view and respond to the world in the same way that God does. Be encouraged: seeing the world from God's perspective is to see Him (Psalm 19). To see Him in His glorious perfections feeds a hunger that drives us to want more of Him. Knowing God is our deepest need and joy (Phil. 3:8; Eph. 3:14-20). Any bit of awe that we have experienced in our life is a shadow and a pointer to something infinitely better in God. When we see a mountain rightly, a sunset rightly, or a person rightly, we begin to see our Creator rightly.

When we see our Creator rightly, we are motivated to live in a way that God intended and created us to live. Our choices and actions in life follow our minds (what we believe) and our hearts (what we love). Spiritual growth requires transformation of our whole being.

Real transformation that moves beyond simple behavioral modification to thinking and acting like Jesus is at the core of what drives us at Journey. We want this for every one of you! As you go through the next few weeks, you will explore the concept of worldview more deeply with your coach. You will seek to clarify your current worldview and consider ways to move toward a more biblical worldview, thereby facilitating movement toward maximum faith. But knowing God more intimately is not an end to itself.

When we grow to know God and love what He loves, we experience a new love for His people like never before.

This new love will allow us to move away from using people for *our* good toward loving them for *their* good. There is great potential for our relationships to improve and grow when God's love is at the center. Even your own ability to receive love from others can be enriched as you experience a growing love from God in Jesus Christ (John 17:26). Your life can truly be different.

How to Use This Book

Just like the first *Journey* series, *Starting the Journey*, you will find that topics are presented in a workbook format. Research shows that when material is only read, about 20% is retained unless you can immediately use what you learned. You don't have to answer all the questions or fill in all the blanks, but those things can help you apply what you are reading. Learning is also increased when we process what we are learning with someone else. That is why the workbooks are best used in a positive coaching-type relationship.

Each of the sessions in this book is designed to follow the related coaching session. Session 1, for instance, can be considered the "homework" to be completed before sitting down with your coach or mentor for your second session. Coaching session 2 will start by reviewing the workbook session 1 together, and then preparation for the workbook session 2. This process continues through the recommended 8 sessions.

It is suggested that coaching sessions last from 1 to 1 ½ hours and then allow sufficient time to complete the homework before the next time you get together. For many, one week between is adequate, and for others two weeks works better. Sometimes the sessions take longer than suggested. We encourage you to respect each other's available time and if it is taking longer than the 1 to 1 ½ hours, consider taking a pause and continuing at the next set time. In this way, it may take more than the stated sessions to get through the material provided.

Worldview Assessment

If you have taken the worldview assessment, you may be anxious to dive in and understand your results, but we ask that you be patient for a bit longer. We need to make sure there is some foundational understanding in place, or we risk the possibility of focusing on our actions alone instead of seeking real heart change.

If you haven't taken the assessment yet, it is important that you do so before going too far in this process as you will gain much more value from each session when you can compare each topic with your personal results.

The Arizona Christian University Worldview Assessment is available at **ACUworldview.com**. Once you complete the online assessment, your personalized report evaluating your worldview will be generated and sent to you by email.

As we move on to the pre-session, keep in mind that this is an invitation to a life-changing journey. In some ways you will be learning new information, but we are also inviting you to enjoy full engagement of yourself as a person. Right information is important, but a growing relationship with God that includes your whole being, mind, heart and will is essential (Matthew 22:37). The biblical worldview is a view of the world through God's eyes. In seeing His perspective, you get to know Him, and knowing Him is "surpassingly greater" than knowing anything else (Philippians 3:8). This will enable us to view the world and others differently—to live more like God designed us to live—to live like Jesus.

Pre-Session – Getting to Know Each Other

You may be wondering, "What is a pre-session?" *Journey toward Maximum Faith* is the second workbook in the Journey Coaching series. If you have gone through *Starting the Journey*, this pre-session will be a valuable review. We encourage you to have that workbook available as you go through *Journey toward Maximum Faith*.

If you haven't gone through *Starting the Journey*, this pre-session will set the foundation for the work we will be doing here.

There are different ways to go through a Journey workbook. Most importantly, we ask that you make this journey a relational one, not a solo learning experience. If someone hasn't invited you to go through this with them, reach out to another person yourself. Think of those people you admire and want to learn from. Perhaps it is someone who has been a believer for a little longer than you have, or someone who has a faith that you want to learn from. As this workbook progresses, there will be discussion about data and information. Still, we want to emphasize that relationships are what bring information to life. There is overwhelming evidence showing that we grow so much more effectively when we study and learn in connection with others. This is probably why Jesus' life was relationship driven. For that reason, *Journey toward Maximum Faith* and the initial series, *Starting the Journey*, were designed to be used in one-on-one or couple-to-couple relationships rather than as independent studies.

Bible-Based

Journey Coaching was developed with a Christian perspective, which teaches us to serve everyone, love everyone, and care for everyone regardless of their worldview, as modeled by Jesus. You don't need to be a Christian to participate in Journey Coaching. We do encourage you to have an openness and curiosity. We ask that you try to build a trusting relationship. As you go through this workbook, you will have many opportunities to compare your existing worldview with the biblical worldview and make decisions about what you believe apart from how the culture and media portray Christians.

If you are going through this workbook with a friend, don't be surprised by your different perspectives. We grow more when we experience life through the eyes of others, especially those who are different from us.

It is important to clarify that coaching is not counseling and is somewhat different from mentoring. In both counseling and mentoring, a person is reaching out to someone who has specific expertise, and the focus is often on problem-solving. If you are meeting with a coach or a friend, consider that this person is on the same journey as you, looking to the expertise that comes from God through His Word, the Bible.

It is important that you feel comfortable sharing with each other. Regardless of where you are on your journey, coaching can help you grow. Most find that they appreciate the opportunity to tell their story to someone else who listens and understands without judgment.

Review from *Starting the Journey*

Getting to Know Each Other

If you've gone through *Starting the Journey*, the following section can be a helpful way to summarize your insights and will be useful as you move forward in *Journey toward Maximum Faith*. If this is your first time together, or if you have not yet gone through the first book, this abbreviated section can provide a great foundation as well.

Stories

This is a good place for the coach to share his/her journey briefly. It may help you to learn how he or she chose to be a part of this process and why he or she feels it is important to be intentional about doing things that will help you grow. Take notes if you would like to remember certain aspects of your coach's story.

Notes from my coach's journey: _______________________

____

____

____

____

____

____

____

____

Next, it is your turn. Share some of the significant events of your life. Consider what people, events, or things have worked to shape you into the person you are today. Some events may have seemed small at the time but ended up being major turning points for you. Also important is identifying what has helped you shape your view of the world and of your perspective of God.

Notes from my journey: _______________________

____

____

____

____

____

____

____

Don't worry if later you think of some things you left out. There will be time to share those in future sessions.

Strengths

Use this space to record the strengths you identified in Session 2 of *Starting the Journey*. If you haven't completed that series yet, consider your story above and reflect on things that stand out that you did well. Remember, characteristics or skills don't have to be perfect to consider them strengths. Why examine strengths? God designed you uniquely. He doesn't want you to stop being you when choosing to follow Jesus. Taking the time to identify your strengths helps you see yourself as part of God's beautiful Creation.

My strengths: ____

____

____

____

____

____

Growth Areas

Use this area to record growth areas you can identify from session 3 of *Starting the Journey* or from reflecting on your own growth areas. Some people call them weaknesses, but we like to define weaknesses as those things we cannot change and need to adapt to, and growth areas as the weaknesses that we have some ability to grow and change if we work hard on them.

My growth areas: (things I could likely change if I worked on them) ____________

____

____

____

____

____

Weaknesses I need to adapt to: (such as chronic illnesses, physical limitations, etc.) __

____

____

____

____

____

Worldview

From *Starting the Journey*, Session 4, what insights did you gain about your personal worldview and how it compares to the biblical worldview? If you haven't completed this part of the first workbook, don't worry. We will have many more discussions about worldview throughout this workbook.

My worldview summary: (from *Starting the Journey*, Session 4) _________________

____

____

____

____

____

____

____

____

Bible as a Roadmap

In Starting the Journey, Session 5, you were introduced to the concept of 10 "stops," identified by Dr. George Barna, that we take along our journey toward full maturity in Christ.

The stops look something like this:

☐ **Stop 1:** Ignorance of the concept or existence of sin.
This is the stop where everybody begins, oblivious to the existence of God or His moral and spiritual standards.

☐ **Stop 2:** Aware of and indifferent to sin.
At this stop, a person becomes aware of the concept of sin but rejects it as a standard to live by.

☐ **Stop 3:** Concern about the implications of personal sin.
At this stop, a person begins to embrace the possibility that sin exists and starts to consider its implications for their life and eternity. They may even begin to pursue or attend a church.

☐ **Stop 4:** Confess sins and ask Jesus Christ to be their Savior.
This stop is where a person confesses themself as a sinner and turns to God for forgiveness in Jesus Christ. For many, their spiritual growth may stall at this point if they believe their prayer for forgiveness is all they need for living the Christian life.

☐ **Stop 5:** Commitment to faith activities.
At this stop, a person's spiritual hunger compels them to get involved with a church and begin to engage in that community's faith activities (i.e., worship services, Christian education classes, personal worship time, and service opportunities).

☐ **Stop 6:** Experience a prolonged period of spiritual discontent.
This stop is where faith activities turn into a set of lifeless rituals and routines that don't feed a growing relationship with God. A new discontent arises that either leads to retreat into continued lifeless rituals or drives them to pursue something more.

☐ **Stop 7:** Experience personal brokenness.
This stop brings someone to a state of brokenness over their deep sin of self-reliance. They realize how much they remain in control and turn to God in confession and repentance.

☐ **Stop 8:** Choose to surrender and submit fully to God.
At this stop a person begins to understand what total surrender, complete submission, and utter dependence on God really means. They begin to allow God to remake their life by giving Him more and more control.

☐ **Stop 9:** Enjoy a profound intimacy with and love for God.
This stop is where someone experiences a new deep and profound experience with God and His love. Life takes on new meaning as each day

is lived in the presence of God with increasing levels of joy, peace, wisdom, and depth of purpose.

- ❑ **Stop 10:** Experience a profound compassion and love for people. This last stop is where a deeper relationship with God allows someone to begin to see people, all people, the way He sees them, to hear them as He hears them, and to love them as He loves them.

In many ways you move through the 10 stops as you move toward a more biblical worldview. We will unpack this in future sessions. If you want, you can read about the 10 stops in Appendix C at the end of this workbook, or by reading Dr. Barna's book, *Maximum Faith*.

At what stop would you consider yourself right now? _______________________________

If you are like most people, you may find that you have progressed to a certain stop and then your faith seemed to stall out, at least for a while. What do you think gets in the way of your growing intimacy with God? _______________________________

____

____

____

Other Insights

If you completed the rest of the *Starting the Journey* sessions (6-7), record here any specific insights you had and share them with your coach.

Session 6 – Planning for Realignment: _______________________________

____

____

____

Session 7 – Follow-up, Support, and Encouragement: _______________________________

____

____

____

How successful were you in accomplishing your stated goals (Session 6 homework)?

____

If not successful, what got in the way? _________________________________

____

____

We commend you for being intentional about joining us on this journey toward maximum faith.

An author of the Bible, the Apostle Paul wrote, "...But one thing I do: forgetting what lies behind and straining forward to what lies ahead, I press on toward the goal for the prize of the upward call of God in Christ Jesus." (Philippians 3:13-14)

Paul was straining toward Jesus, who is God in the flesh. Exploring your own worldview with a trusted person and striving to understand how it compares with God's view in the Bible is the most worthwhile task you could ever be intentional about. It is our hope and prayer that you look to this Journey with anticipation and hope for what God can do in your life.

Homework

If you haven't taken the worldview assessment yet, it is important that you do so before the next (first) session.

The Arizona Christian University Worldview Assessment is available at: **ACUworldview.com**. Once you complete the assessment, your worldview results will be sent to you by email.

SESSION | One

Understanding Worldview

Understanding Worldview

Here we go—the journey begins. Like any journey it is important to have some idea of where you are going and how you will get there. So, since our journey is taking you to a deeper understanding of how you view the world (i.e., your worldview), it is important to ensure that you have the best possible understanding of the concept of worldview.

What Is Worldview?

Let's start at the beginning. Even if someone has spent their lifetime attending church, they may not realize that they have a specific view of the world, know where it came from, or understand how they can adjust it. Our worldview, or the way we view the world around us, is a set of beliefs we create and utilize that help us make sense of our world. Everyone has one, it is part of how we survive. You can think of it as set of lenses or glasses that you look through to interpret reality. In fact, we rarely see reality or the world around us without filtering it through our worldview lens.

Your worldview is not merely a set of beliefs disengaged from your behavior. Your worldview, based on those beliefs, also determines how you respond to the world. That is because most circumstances in life are largely neutral. It is the way you think about any situation that helps you determine whether it is primarily good or bad. Every decision you make is determined by your worldview. It influences your goals, values, morals, faith, identity, finances, relationship, and even lifestyle choices. Your worldview is the accumulation of your key beliefs, and these beliefs will determine how you behave. In this way our choices are predictable and manageable.

Take, for example, an election. The reality is that one person won, and the others didn't. Whether this seems like a good or bad thing, or whether you believe the election was fair or not, depends on your worldview and how the particular lens you look through influences the way you think and feel. When we are oblivious to the concept of worldview, it is likely we will have an expectation that everyone does or should see the world in the same way we do, causing many potential conflicts in our relationships. The conflicts often come as a result of seeing other's behavior through our own worldview. It kind of goes like this: "I wouldn't vote that way unless I didn't know better, therefore that person is ignorant."

How Worldview is Formed

We start forming our worldview in infancy as we explore the environment around us and learn how things work. A small baby sitting in her highchair lets go of a toy and it falls to the ground. She is surprised at first, but then she becomes curious. She tries it with another toy, and then another. Before long she is laughing as it becomes a fun game until she is out of toys. Then she cries. If the adults in her life interact with her by picking up the toys and putting them back on her tray, she learns another truth about her world. She starts forming the belief that if she lets let go of something, it falls, and if she cries someone will pick it up and give it back to her.

Our worldview starts very small and simple, then expands as we grow and mature. At first our home seems to be the whole world, then we have other experiences such as getting to know extended family, church, school, and friends. Our view of the world expands from believing that all families are pretty much like ours, to finding that others don't live exactly the same way we do. In fact, they see and do many things differently. All of this becomes information for our curious minds to ponder. In some cases, we take new information in and change our view of the world slightly. In other situations, we might decide that the way others do things is "wrong" and our preferred worldview or value system is "right." In that case, our view of the world would stay fairly consistent and in time could become quite rigid.

Think back over your own life. Can you remember some of the ways you thought about the world around you when you were very young that are different than how you see them today? ____

____

____

____

What (or who) caused your view of the world to change? _________________________

____

Our worldview affects our value system, our attitudes, behaviors, and actions. There are so many things that influence how we view the world and what we value. Our parents, grandparents, other caregivers, teachers, mentors, and peers all have influence over these things as we mature. Usually by adulthood we are exposed to many different lifestyles and beliefs. Along the way we begin to make decisions about whether to reject or integrate the different views of the world into our own. We face a major tension when someone we value presents a worldview that is in complete opposition to ours. In fact, one of the biggest challenges of adolescence happens when the views they held as children (which are often identical to parental views), are challenged by peers or educators. Peer pressure on one side and family pressure on the other causes teens to experience a great deal of stress, which they cope within a variety of ways. By this age their brain has gone through a major reorganization that allows them to think more abstractly. The child who used to ask "Why?" in order to understand how the world works, is now the teen who wants to know "Why does it have to be that way?" Usually, to parent's dismay, they begin questioning the rules and values they grew up with.

Even if we are not religious, our worldview still must address many of the same questions such as: "How did we get here?" (origin) and "Why are we here?" (purpose), as well as "How do we determine right from wrong, good from bad?" (morality). Morality also includes concepts such as forgiveness, poverty, injustice, and suffering. As stated before, everyone has a worldview and here are some worldview questions to start you thinking.

What does your worldview say about pain and suffering? _______________________

____

____

____

____

What gives you value as an individual? What takes it away? _______________________

____

____

____

____

You will have a lot more opportunities to explore your own worldview in future sessions. These questions are offered to help you begin the thinking process about worldview in general.

Getting More Specific—How a Biblical Worldview Develops

The most important thing to explore in our worldview is how it compares to God's view of the world. Think back to how you began to explore a belief (or disbelief) in the God of the Bible. Whether you were raised in a Christian home and attended church every Sunday, or came from a non-believing home and were invited to attend church events with a friend, you likely came to a point where you started wondering "Is this true?" And then you begin to wrestle with some of life's biggest questions for yourself. For instance: what do you believe about how you got here and what happens after you die? If you determine that you are not here by accident, then why are you here? What is your purpose for living?

Can you remember how your Christian journey started? _______________________

____

____

____

____

Who were some significant people that influenced your early spiritual development?

____

____

____

____

Understanding Your Arizona Christian University Assessment Results

When you receive the Arizona Christian University Worldview Assessment, the first score you see will reflect your overall personal worldview. This will be identified as either a biblical worldview or one of the common competing worldviews. The next section will break out five major categories that make up your overall worldview. Your scores related to each category will place you in one of three segments: World Citizen, Emergent Follower, or Integrated Disciple. It is possible to have a biblical worldview overall and still have a competing worldview in one of the main categories. It is even more common to have a biblical worldview in one or two categories but lack a biblical worldview as your dominant philosophy of life.

World Citizen – No discernible biblical worldview (82% of American adults). This would include stops 1–3 on the 10 stops from *Maximum Faith* (see Appendix C).

Emerging Follower – Portions of the biblical worldview, but not fully developed into comprehensive biblical worldviewis would include stops 4–7 on the 10 stops from *Maximum Faith*.

Integrated Disciple – Possesses a fully developed and integrated biblical worldview reflected in both beliefs and behaviors (4% of American adults). This would include stops 7-10 on the 10 stops from *Maximum Faith*.

Biblical Worldview Categories

Let's begin focusing on some specific biblical worldview categories so we can better understand what a scriptural view of the world looks like. Our goal with this session is not to explore your own beliefs regarding these categories. We will do that in the next session. At this point, we simply want to look at the key categories that make up a God-view of the world from the Bible. This will help us compare our view of the world with God's and see where we might discard beliefs that are not consistent with biblical teaching and replace them with those that are.

The following chart provides basic definitions of the categories used throughout this workbook. It will be helpful to become familiar with them for future reference.

Categories	Definitions
Bible, Truth, and Morals	What you believe about the Bible and how it affects your behavior, your perspectives on the concept and pursuit of truth, and your ideas about discerning right from wrong and what that looks like in practice
Faith Practices	How you apply what you believe about the Bible. How you put those perspectives into practice. Includes beliefs and activity related to evangelism, worship, prayer, confession, and spiritual growth; and how you handle purpose, temptation, and sin
God, Creation, and History	What you believe about the existence, nature, and work of the God of Israel, the Trinity, Satan, and the meaning of world history
Lifestyle, Behavior, and Relationships	Your perspectives related to your lifestyle activities and preferences, how you interact with resources and opportunities, and the nature and goal of your interpersonal relationships
Sin, Salvation, and Your God Relationship	How you think about and address sin, your beliefs and choices related to personal salvation, and the nature and pursuit of your relationship with God
Family, Value of Life, Human Character & Nature, Purpose & Calling	*These make up the sixth category of items included in the overall assessment results. However, you will not see individual category results for them.* A series of crucial worldview factors that are not reported individually but as a group of factors. This includes perspectives about marriage, children, and family, as well as the value and dignity of life. Also includes the purpose and calling for each human being, and the nature and character components of every individual. These areas are part of a person's overall worldview. The biblical worldview perspective for understanding these factors is found in Scripture.

The next session in this workbook is aimed at understanding your current worldview and how it aligns with or deviates from a biblical worldview. This is the first step that must be taken to move toward a more biblical worldview. With your coach, you will grow to understand God more deeply, thus being better able to see the world as He sees it and in turn live as He designed you.

Have you had any fears about discovering your current worldview or about moving it toward a more Biblical one? ____

____

____

____

Homework

If you have not had an opportunity to complete the worldview assessment and receive your assessment results prior to starting this workbook and coaching process, it is important that you do so now before the next session.

The Arizona Christian University Worldview Assessment is available at **ACUworldview.com**. Once you complete the online assessment, your personalized report evaluating your worldview will be generated and sent to you by email.

SESSION | # Two

Making Sense of Your Personal Worldview

Making Sense of Your Personal Worldview

The worldview assessment could be one of the most important things you do for yourself this year! You might think of it as GPS for your faith and relationship with God. Picture yourself driving across the country. After a few hours, you take a break and then jump back on the interstate highway. Without GPS or even a map, you could get lost or maybe drive for hours before realizing that you were heading the wrong way.

One family was driving through the upper peninsula of Michigan a few years ago, looking for some of the amazing waterfalls that can be seen in that part of the country. Unfortunately, there were very few cell towers, so the phone's navigation app was useless. This traveler stopped to ask directions, but the well-meaning local gave non-specific directions that were of little help. This seems to be the way a lot of people navigate their spiritual journey. They have limited understanding about the Bible themselves, while getting information from others who also have limited information. For this reason, the Arizona Christian University Worldview Assessment can be like the GPS app redirecting a weary traveler.

When you first read through your overall worldview assessment score, what reaction(s) did you have?

- ☐ No surprises
- ☐ Happy
- ☐ Shocked
- ☐ Disappointed
- ☐ Confused
- ☐ Embarrassed
- ☐ Other _________________________

Explain your reaction above: ____

____

____

In this session, we begin a process intended to lead you to the exploration of your own personal worldview. As you understand your own worldview, change becomes possible. You can then compare it to a biblical worldview, to learn what modifications, if any, need to take place. This may feel a bit scary, but there is nothing better than growing to see the world the way God sees it. So, grab your favorite Bible translation and keep it open beside this workbook as you study. If you do not have a Bible or study Bible and are wondering how to choose among them all, Appendix E near the end of this workbook will help.

It may feel uncomfortable if you find out that you believe something that doesn't line up with biblical teaching, but we encourage you to try to look at this revelation as a good thing. If your hope and goal is to see the world as God sees it, then it is imperative that you know specifically what beliefs and behaviors must change to be able to think like Jesus. If you remain unaware of how your beliefs are misaligned, you may never reach your goal of growing toward maximum faith. Your inaccurate thinking about God will remain and it will cause you to live inconsistently with who God made you to be. Being a disciple of Jesus Christ is not like taking part in a short-term certification program. It is making a lifelong commitment to learning and growing to become more and more like Jesus, viewing the world and caring for others as He does.

As we have seen already, your worldview shapes the way you live and relate to others. If you say you believe something, yet live in a way that contradicts it, what does that really mean? The root for the English word "believe" could also be understood as "to love or to live." This means that what you believe can be identified by how you live. If you believe it is wrong to lie but fudge on your income tax, somewhere deep inside you don't really believe it is always wrong to lie. Our beliefs are always aligned with our behaviors, although sometimes at an unconscious level. If they were not so aligned, we would be in a state of cognitive dissonance, struggling with ourselves. In fact, when we go through the transformation process, the episodes of dissonance we wrestle with are evidence that a significant change is taking place within us.

Being honest, under what circumstances do you believe it is okay to lie? _________

____

____

____

Under what circumstances would it be okay for someone to lie to you? ____________

____

____

____

Answering these questions can help identify a small part of how we view the world. Most people would have fewer exceptions for others lying to them than for their own "little white lies." Let's go a little deeper.

Jack (not his real name) was very vocal about his faith in Jesus, evangelizing to co-workers, customers, and vendors every chance he got. Yet, Jack also was very well known for being rude, even abusive, to anyone who disagreed with him. It was clear that he believed in God's truth, but not so much in God's grace.

If your co-workers knew or found out that you were a follower of Jesus, what do you think they might assume about your beliefs? ________________________________

____

____

If this last question made you uncomfortable, process that discomfort with your coach. ____

____

____

Now let's turn to examining your assessment results.

By the time you are reading this part of the workbook, it is important that you have already taken the worldview assessment and received your results. If you have not, we suggest you take a break to do so now.

The Arizona Christian University Worldview Assessment is available at **ACUworldview.com**. Once you complete the online assessment, your personalized report evaluating your worldview will be generated and sent to you by email.

Exploring Your Arizona Christian University Worldview Assessment

This is a good place to pull out your Arizona Christian University Worldview Assessment Report. It will look something like the following sample.

NOTE: Your report's national norms might be different than these. National norms can change over time, and are recalculated as new national research is conducted.

ARIZONA CHRISTIAN
UNIVERSITY

WORLDVIEW ASSESSMENT

From Dr. George Barna and the Cultural Research Center at Arizona Christian University

You scored strong...

BIBLICAL WORLDVIEW

Module Scores

BIBLICAL WORLDVIEW

Bible, Truth and Morals
INTEGRATED DISCIPLE

This series of questions examined what you believe about the Bible and how it affects your behavior; your perspectives on the concept and pursuit of truth; and your ideas about discerning right and wrong (i.e., morality), and what that looks like in practice.

NATIONAL NORMS:
12% INTEGRATED DISCIPLES
13% EMERGENT FOLLOWERS
76% WORLD CITIZENS

In this next table we are going to look at where you landed within those major categories that make up a biblical worldview. Summarize the results of your assessment in the right column of the table. Then spend some time talking with each other about your individual results in each category.

Category	Topics	Your Results
1	**Bible, Truth, and Morals**	☐ Integrated Disciple ☐ Emergent Follower ☐ World Citizen
2	**Faith Practices**	☐ Integrated Disciple ☐ Emergent Follower ☐ World Citizen
3	**God, Creation, and History**	☐ Integrated Disciple ☐ Emergent Follower ☐ World Citizen
4	**Lifestyle, Behavior, and Relationships**	☐ Integrated Disciple ☐ Emergent Follower ☐ World Citizen
5	**Sin, Salvation, and Your God Relationship**	☐ Integrated Disciple ☐ Emergent Follower ☐ World Citizen
6	**Family, Value of Life, Human Character & Nature, and Purpose & Calling**	You will not find a break-out score listed for this category. Items from this section are a part of the overall worldview assessment that we will explore further as we go

Which, if any, of these results seem surprising? _______________________________

____

Which results, if any, are confusing to you? _________________________________

____

____

____

Individual results can be troublesome even if someone has been a Christian for many years, and especially for those who are possibly working or serving in a church or Christian organization. But take heart, the goal of this assessment is not to criticize or condemn anyone. It is to provide information for the purpose of discipleship and growth toward a more mature relationship with Jesus and others.

If your results in the categories above did not turn out the way you expected or wanted, what was your initial response? (check all that apply)

- ❑ I was upset, maybe even angry.
- ❑ I thought, "This can't be right, there must be something wrong with the assessment."
- ❑ I felt guilt or shame.
- ❑ I was confused about how I could have gotten things so messed up.
- ❑ I felt gratitude. I now see why my Christian walk may have become stale and unfulfilling.
- ❑ Other: ____

Another part of your Arizona Christian University Worldview Report shows how you score related to the *Seven Cornerstones of a Biblical Worldview* as identified in Dr. Barna's research work. These cornerstones refer to particular beliefs and commitments that serve as a foundation for someone to develop a consistently biblical life in thought and action. Without all seven of these in place, it is difficult, if not impossible, to see the world as God sees it. That is why it is so important to explore how your beliefs compare to God's Word, which reflects His view of the world.

	Cornerstone	Your Score
1	An orthodox, biblical understanding of God.	
2	All human beings are sinful by nature; every choice we make has moral contours and consequences.	
3	Jesus Christ is the sole means to individual salvation, accomplished through our acknowledgment and confession of our sins and complete reliance on His grace for the forgiveness of those sins.	
4	The entire Bible is true, reliable, and relevant, making it the best moral guide for every person, in all situations.	
5	Absolute moral truth exists, and those truths are defined by God, described in the Bible and unchanging across time and cultures.	
6	The ultimate purpose of human life is to know, love, and serve God with all your heart, mind, strength, and soul.	
7	Success on Earth is best understood as consistent obedience to God—in thoughts, words, and actions.	

Phew, this can be a lot to take in! The Arizona Christian University Worldview Assessment in some ways is like having just gone through a chest X-ray. But instead of looking at your physical body, this one is giving you vital information about the condition of your spiritual heart. It may be just as hard to find out your spiritual heart is unhealthy as it would be to find out your physical heart needs medical attention. Either one would be risky to ignore!

If you found out from a medical exam that your heart was not functioning as it should, would you consider doing whatever it takes to fix it, even going in for surgery? ☐ Yes ☐ No

Why/Why not? ____

____

____

If you just found out that your worldview, which is reflective of your spiritual heart, is unhealthy in some ways, are you willing to look at what you might be able to do to make some changes?   ☐ Yes   ☐ No

Why/Why not? ____

____

____

Comparing Your Beliefs to Actions

Believing the right things is only part of what is involved in living and becoming like Jesus. He didn't stop at just believing rightly. Jesus lived out His beliefs in everything He did. His view of the world was evident in every conversation He had, no matter whom He was talking to.

Reflecting on your daily life choices and actions, how consistent are they with your beliefs in each of the five categories measured in the assessment? ______________

____

____

____

____

This next section will help you identify more about your personal worldview as it applies to the measured categories. All the categories are included in the overall score, although you should have received individual scores for only 1–5. The sixth category is still a very important part of your overall score, so we have included information about it below.

Category #1: Bible, Truth, and Morals

This category examines what you believe about the Bible and how it affects your behavior, your perspectives on the concept and pursuit of truth, and your ideas about discerning right and wrong (i.e., morality), and what that looks like in practice.

Any discussion of biblical content, truth, and morals must first address the question of the authority and authenticity of the Bible as God's Word. If we are in any way dismissive or unsure of the Bible's authority, we will struggle to follow its truth and moral guidelines. In what ways do you believe this to be true or untrue, and what significance does the Bible have regarding the way you live your life? _______________

____

____

____

____

____

Explain how you understand the concept of truth. (Is there anything you can say is true with absolute certainty?) ____

____

____

____

____

Think about the nature of moral behavior. How do you identify right vs. wrong? Good vs. bad? ____

____

____

____

____

How does the way you live your life reflect your beliefs about the Bible, truth, and morals? ____

____

____

____

____

Category #2: Faith Practices

This includes beliefs and activity related to evangelism, worship, prayer, confession, and spiritual growth, as well as purpose, temptation, and sin.

How important has the growth of your faith and relationship with God been over the last few years?

- ❑ Not important
- ❑ Somewhat important
- ❑ Very important. If so, what things have you been intentionally doing to continue growing? ____
____

Which of the following faith activities do you practice on a regular basis?

- ❑ Reading, studying, and/or meditating on the Bible
- ❑ Prayer
- ❑ Confession
- ❑ Worship
- ❑ Fellowship and community
- ❑ Service
- ❑ Stewardship
- ❑ Fasting (giving up an earthly appetite to develop a stronger appetite for God)
- ❑ Journaling (recording prayers, thoughts, study notes, etc.)
- ❑ Other ____

How do you respond to temptation? What, if anything, do you usually do when you become aware of your own sin? ____
____
____

How does your life reflect these beliefs on a daily basis? ____
____
____

Category #3: God, Creation, and History

This series of questions examines what you believe about the existence, nature, and work of the God of Israel, the Trinity, Satan, and the meaning of world history.

What does your worldview, in relation to the elements included in this category, say about how you got here? Where did your beliefs in this area come from? _________

____

____

____

____

Who or what is in control of this world? Is anyone or anything in control? How much control do you possess? ____

____

____

____

How does your worldview, related to the elements in this category, affect the way you cope with things like death or sickness? ________________________________

____

____

____

Looking at this category of beliefs, how do your actions and behaviors line up? _____

____

____

____

____

Category #4: Lifestyle, Behavior, and Relationships

This module of questions explores your perspectives related to your lifestyle activities and preferences, how you interact with resources and opportunities, and the nature and goal of your interpersonal relationships.

How does your worldview affect the decisions you make on a day-to-day basis? ____

____

____

____

____

How does it shape your use of money and other resources? _______________

____

____

____

____

How does your worldview impact your relationships with people (friends, co-workers, acquaintances, those you don't know, etc.)? _______________

____

____

____

____

____

Looking at this category of beliefs, how consistent are your actions and behaviors with your beliefs? _______________

____

____

____

____

Category #5: Sin, Salvation, and Your God Relationship

This module includes questions regarding how you think about and address sin, your beliefs and choices related to personal salvation, and the nature and pursuit of your relationship with God.

What does the term "sin" mean to you? What emotions does it generate? _________

____

____

____

____

How do you address concepts of forgiveness and reconciliation? Are you as forgiving to others as you would like or expect them to be toward you? ____________________

____

____

____

____

____

Given that we all sin and fall short of God's plan for us, how can anyone get to Heaven? What do you have to do to get there? ____________________________________

____

____

____

____

Looking at this category of beliefs, how do your actions and behaviors line up? ______

____

____

____

____

____

Category #6: Family, Value of Life, Human Character and Nature, Purpose and Calling

A series of crucial worldview factors that are not reported individually but as a group of factors. This includes perspectives about marriage, children, and family, as well as the value and dignity of life. It also includes the purpose and calling for each human being, and the nature and character components of every individual. These areas are part of a person's overall worldview. The biblical worldview perspective for understanding these factors is found in Scripture.

Note: You will not find a breakout score listed for this category, but items from this section are a part of the overall worldview assessment.

What gives a person value as an individual? What diminishes it? __________________

____

____

How does your worldview influence the way you look at issues such as abortion and euthanasia? ____

____

____

What does your worldview say about poverty, injustice, and suffering? What causes them, and what can be done about them? ______________________________________

____

____

Looking at this category of beliefs, how do your actions and behaviors line up? ______

____

____

____

Once you've reflected on these six categories, have a conversation with your coach about any differences or similarities between your beliefs and actions.

As you are coming to a better understanding of your own personal worldview, our next session will be focused on why a biblical worldview is essential for spiritual and personal growth.

SESSION | # Three

Why a Biblical Worldview Is Essential

Why a Biblical Worldview Is Essential for Growing toward Maximum Faith

Now that you can better understand the concept of a worldview and your own personal worldview, you can begin the process of determining how yours can be more aligned with God's view of the world. The goal of this session is to help you better understand a biblical worldview and how it can help you grow.

So, let's begin by thinking more deeply about a biblical worldview. The Bible teaches that God created the world, including you, with a purpose (Jeremiah 29:11). The One who creates also defines the way Creation was designed to operate. Having a biblical worldview, then, is essentially striving to see ourselves and the world as God the Creator intended it to be seen. We can see things the way He sees them because He revealed them in the Bible.

You can think of the Bible as an owner's manual of sorts. Consider, for example, the car you drive to work. Usually in the glove compartment or online you will find the owner's manual for your car. The designers and makers of your vehicle didn't expect that you would automatically know the best way to handle and maintain it, so they made a reference available. It is a resource where you will find things like intended use for the vehicle and warnings about how you will invalidate the warranty if you use it in a way that was not intended.

For instance, if your car has a towing capacity of only 1,000 pounds it's not a good idea to try to pull a 10,000-pound trailer. You may be able to go down the road with it for a while but will likely cause some serious damage to your car, and maybe to yourself, by using it in a way that wasn't intended. Or, can you imagine deciding to use your Toyota Prius as a snowplow? That would probably end in disaster. The Toyota manufacturer had a specific use in mind for that car design and it most likely wasn't built for heavy labor.

In the same way we need our all-knowing and all-powerful God to teach and guide us. He did so in the most spectacular way through the birth, life, and death of His Son, Jesus Christ.

Seen in this way, the Bible is not just a set of arbitrary rules. It holds a wealth of information designed to help us see the world through God's perspective and live the life He designed for us. That is why a biblical worldview is so important. No one can understand how to rightly view the world better than its Creator. So, it is crucial that we measure our view of the world with what God has revealed in the Bible.

The Bible gives us more than a right view of the world; it provides a right view of God. Knowing Him rightly and living in a restored relationship with Him is the greatest experience any human could ever have. It is what we were made for. God's greatest revelation of Himself came in His coming as a human in Jesus Christ. He embodied the perfect worldview. He lived it out before all of humanity and we have it historically recorded in the Bible. Without our Creator defining our worldview, we would be left to figure it out for ourselves. Human history shows the futility of that endeavor.

It is very important to understand that having a biblical worldview and living it out through every aspect of our lives is crucial if we want to move towards experiencing maximum faith. When we begin to see the world as God sees it, and integrate that perspective into every aspect of our lives, we become an integrated disciple of Christ. That integration of faith into every dimension of life is what enables us to move toward maximum faith.

The bottom line is that worldview matters because every decision you make is based on that perspective. Your life experience and influence are the sum total of your decisions every moment of every day. You must begin by learning to think like Christ in order to be able to live like Him.

Why We Can Trust the Bible

You may be thinking, "This is all fine and good, but how can I know that the Bible is actually the inspired Word of God? Wasn't it just written by ordinary people?" Let's look at what we can know about the Bible:

- Scholars have affirmed that it is the most well-verified, attested to, historically accurate book in the history of the world.

- There are 66 unique books in the Bible, written by different authors over thousands of years, yet there is an overall unity and harmony across the whole Bible that can only be explained as being guided by the Holy Spirit through the whole process.

- We have only one Bible, but many different versions of it. The Bible was originally written in three languages: Hebrew, Aramaic, and Greek. Because most people do not read these languages, the Bible has been translated into hundreds of languages all over the globe.

- Current Bible versions were translated directly from the original three languages.

- History is essentially God's story describing the unfolding of His eternal plan, and the Bible is His unique and special documentation of the meaning of history for humankind. It is developed in three major themes: Creation, humankind's fall, and humanity's redemption by God. We can see the story developing from the account of the creation of the world, the severe effects of sin, and God's loving solution through the provision of the Savior/ Messiah. Each of the books throughout the Old Testament anticipates His coming, while the books of the New Testament describe His impact.

- Jesus fulfilled over 300 prophecies that were written long before He was born. Some identify where and when He was to be born, something He could never have had anything to do with.

- There were hundreds of witnesses to the death of Jesus who were still alive when the Gospel records were being written.

- There are many historical writings outside the Bible that corroborate many of the stories surrounding the life and death of Jesus, as well as other historical facts.

- There were hundreds of eyewitnesses to seeing Jesus alive after He died on the cross. Many of them who had gone into hiding at Jesus' death were willing to risk their own death by testifying that Jesus was seen alive again.

- Time and time again, archaeologists have discovered places and verified time periods for events and locations identified in the Bible.

When you research the authenticity and reliability of the Bible, it is clear that there was a superpower (the Holy Spirit) overriding the process! If you want more information about this, check out the helpful links in the References page in the back of this workbook.

Let's take a moment to review:

Why is a biblical worldview so important? _______________________________________

____

____

What might be some possible consequences of living outside of a biblical worldview?

____

____

____

How Our Worldview Changes over Time

Our view of the world isn't stagnant but changes over time. These changes can bring us closer to a right relationship with God or pull us away from it. There are many ways that this can happen. Let's begin by looking at some of the common examples.

Our view of the world changes **as our thinking ability matures**. When we are very young, our brains are only able to process in a concrete or literal thinking way. By adolescence, we begin to be able to think and reason more abstractly. This enables us to comprehend complex patterns, analogies, and metaphors. To better understand this, imagine a small child who was told to show her sister "the ropes" in her new classroom. Unable to understand the abstract reasoning, she began to cry "We don't have any ropes!" In time, as she matured, this girl was able to realize that "show her the ropes" is a metaphor for helping someone get acquainted with a new environment.

Our worldview changes as **we learn new information**. No one in all of history has had the overwhelming volume of information available to them that we do today. But fake news has been around for generations. It just means we have to be even more discerning than our ancestors and remember that not all new information is true or helpful. Our great-grandparents had to watch out for snake oil salesmen who sold lies and misinformation for the purpose of separating naïve and hurting people from their hard-earned money.

Misinformation will pull us away from seeing the world from God's view if we aren't careful. One way to combat misleading information is to compare it with what God's Word says about a subject. The best way to do that is to be constantly reading His Word. Even if you have already read the Bible from Genesis to Revelation, reading it again and again will allow the Holy Spirit to teach you new insights that relate to the relationships and life experiences you are dealing with at the time.

Going through different **life experiences** will undoubtedly alter your view of the world. Many young people begin questioning the values and beliefs they learned at home once they are introduced to new experiences and ideas in school or college. One way to counter that is to consider going on mission trips or youth Bible study opportunities. Studying abroad or finding ways to experience cultures different than ours can broaden our view of the world considerably and keep us from having a limited view of the world.

Social interactions also influence our worldview development. It is a basic human need to fit in and be accepted. When peers point out your different perspective in a negative way, it can cause you to question and sometimes change your values and beliefs. If you attend church with your friends or family and find it valuable, but then a different group of peers tells you only narrow-minded people believe all that stuff, it can cause you to question if you are right or they are. This is what Jesus was talking about (Matthew 13:23) when He told the parable about the good seed falling among weeds that grew up and choked it out. Jesus was emphasizing the effect of people and circumstances on our developing Biblical worldview.

Pain, trauma, and grief are often circumstances that can cause us to either move towards a biblical worldview or push away from it. If something painful happens to us, it may act as a challenge to our biblical worldview or it might shine a light on some incorrect belief or misunderstanding of who God really is. If our belief is that God would not let bad things happen to His people, then how do we make sense of the fact that bad things do happen to us. A biblical worldview shows us over and over that God uses even painful circumstances for the good of His people.

How has your worldview changed over time? _______________________________

____

____

____

____

What has caused those changes to your worldview? _______________________

____

____

____

____

Now that we understand why having a biblical worldview is important, in the next session we will start looking at those main categories to see where your worldview aligns with a biblical worldview. We do this first, because understanding your alignment in any area can help you acknowledge and work on areas where you differ from a biblical worldview.

SESSION | **Four**

Where You Align with a

Biblical Worldview –

Strengths

Where You Align with a Biblical Worldview

Can you imagine the goodness of God in sharing Himself, His character, creativity, power, wisdom, and ways with us? We were created in His image. Let that sink in for a moment. Reflecting His image allows us the ability to see and fully appreciate Him and all He has made. This is true worship; to be able to see all that He has made, and by extension to be able to see Him in it (Romans 1:19–20). This is a wonder beyond belief.

Just as God shows Himself through His Creation, even more so He reveals His nature through His Word, the Bible. By looking at both, we can begin to identify ways we align with a biblical worldview, God's view. We can see things as they were created and see the Creator in them. What a gift from God! In whatever way you are already aligned with a biblical worldview, you can give thanks to God.

In this session, we will focus on your areas of alignment with a biblical worldview. We will explore how you got there so that you might continue to grow. We will focus on each area in order that you might solidify your view and take it deeper. We will also encourage you to look at your choices and actions, which demonstrate the ways you are living out a biblical worldview day to day. As discussed earlier, your actions and choices reflect your true worldview. So, we want to ensure that your worldview is not merely cognitive but has moved into your heart and is guiding your behavior.

Let's identify your alignment in the different categories below. Reviewing the results from your worldview assessment, record on the following table where your view of the world and way of living is in alignment with the biblical worldview categories. If your Arizona Christian University Assessment results indicate you scored as an Integrated Disciple in any or all the categories, the following exercise will help you take a deeper dive.

In the areas that you identify as an Integrated Disciple, this means that your beliefs and actions in those categories align significantly with a biblical worldview. Think of knowing God as a journey, not a destination. While we can't fully understand how

God views our world, we can continue to grow to know Him better throughout our lives.

Category	Topics	Areas of Alignment (Record below the categories where you scored as an Integrated Disciple)
1	Bible, Truth, and Morals	
2	Faith Practices	
3	God, Creation, and History	
4	Lifestyle, Behavior, and Relationships	
5	Sin, Salvation, and the God Relationship	
6	Family, Value of Life, Human Character & Nature, and Purpose & Calling	

Were there areas of alignment that surprised you? Why? _______________________

____

____

What might you do to continue growing in your areas of alignment? _____________

____

____

____

Take time right now to celebrate God's grace in allowing you to glimpse the world the way He does. Describe this experience: ________________________________

____

____

____

You can have great confidence that you are looking at the world correctly when your view of the world matches God's view, as taught in the Bible. So, you can know when you view things rightly, the way God intended them to be viewed, when your view aligns with Scripture.

This creates the further possibility of relating to God more naturally and frequently. It allows people to understand themselves, to relate to others, and to think of the world rightly. It provides the opportunity to live the way God created you to live. You can live in a right relationship with Him, knowing His loving presence and intention for you and all things.

Benefits of Sharing God's View of the World

While God doesn't promise us a trouble-free life, there are so many amazing benefits of living in line with God's worldview and striving to grow toward maximum faith. Things like:

- **We can experience the power of the Holy Spirit –** God promises "The Helper" will be with Jesus' followers to give wisdom, courage, and strength.

  - *"... and I will ask the Father, and He will give you another Helper, to be with you forever, even the Spirit of truth, whom the world cannot receive, because it neither sees Him nor knows Him. You know Him, for He dwells with you and will be in you."* (John 14:15-17)

  - *"When the Spirit of truth comes, he will guide you into all the truth, for he will not speak on his own authority, but whatever he hears he will speak, and he will declare to you the things that are to come."* (John 16:13)

- **Our thinking and attitude begins to shift –** When we start to see people, things, and events differently, our attitude toward them changes. When we acknowledge God owns everything, for instance, we feel differently about money. Instead of asking, "How much of our money do we need to give to God?" it becomes, "How much of God's money should we spend on ourselves?" When we see others as being loved by God, we may feel compassion and concern instead of frustration and irritation when they need something from us.

  - *"Do not be conformed to this world, but be transformed by the renewal of your mind, that by testing you may discern what is the will of God, what is good and acceptable and perfect."* (Romans 12:2)

  - *"Finally, brothers, whatever is true, whatever is honorable, whatever is just, whatever is pure, whatever is lovely, whatever is commendable, if there is any excellence, if there is anything worthy of praise, think about these things. What you have learned[e] and received and heard and seen in me—practice these things, and the God of peace will be with you."* (Philippians 4:8-9).

- **We begin to produce the fruit of the Spirit -** This is evidence of the Holy Spirit facilitating growth in us. In John 15:1-11, we see a description of Jesus as the vine, and us as the branches. Apart from the vine, branches cannot produce fruit. The "fruit of the spirit" is comprised of those things that He produces through us, not things we work hard to produce on our own.

  - *"But the fruit of the Spirit is love, joy, peace, patience, kindness, goodness, faithfulness, gentleness, self-control; against such things there is no law."* (Galatians 5:22-23)

- **The quality of our relationships may improve –** Our relationships change when we start loving people as God does, and not just those who are loveable in our eyes. When we regard another person as a beloved child of God, instead of seeing their flaws we see their value. Our attitude toward them softens. We start to see them through eyes of compassion, and it encourages us to be more honest and transparent with one another.

- *"This is my commandment, that you love one another as I have loved you."* (John 15:12)

- *"So whatever you wish that others would do to you, do also to them, for this is the Law and the Prophets."* (Matthew 7:12)

- *"But I say to you who hear, Love your enemies, do good to those who hate you, bless those who curse you, pray for those who abuse you … Judge not, and you will not be judged; condemn not, and you will not be condemned; forgive, and you will be forgiven; give, and it will be given to you. Good measure, pressed down, shaken together, running over, will be put into your lap. For with the measure, you use it will be measured back to you."* (Luke 6:27-28 & 37-38)

- **We can increase in fulfillment of work and service –** Work wasn't the result of the fall or a punishment; it is a God-given pursuit designed for our own benefit before the fall. Just as God worked when He created the world, He created us in His image. To work and be creative is to reflect God's nature to the world.

  - *"Whatever you do, work heartily, as for the Lord and not for men,"* (Colossians 3:23)

  - *"I perceived that there is nothing better for them than to be joyful and to do good as long as they live; also that everyone should eat and drink and take pleasure in all his toil—this is God's gift to man."* (Ecclesiastes 3:12-13)

- **We may find increased physical and emotional health –** When we see the world through God's perspective, our fears and anxieties are reduced. When we trust God even in difficult situations, our levels of stress hormones decrease and our bodies are more at peace.

- *"Therefore I tell you, do not be anxious about your life, what you will eat or what you will drink, nor about your body, what you will put on. Is not life more than food, and the body more than clothing? Look at the birds of the air: they neither sow nor reap nor gather into barns, and yet your heavenly Father feeds them. Are you not of more value than they?"* (Matthew 6:25-26)

- *"The righteous flourish like the palm tree and grow like a cedar in Lebanon. They are planted in the house of the Lord; they flourish in the courts of our God. They still bear fruit in old age; they are ever full of sap and green."* (Psalm 92:12-14).

Word of Caution

We would like to offer a warning about the temptation to become prideful or feel superior to others when we find areas of alignment with the biblical worldview. There is no one with a perfect biblical worldview except Jesus. We all fall short in some ways. Likewise, in areas where we see misalignment the temptation can be to feel shame or self-condemnation. It helps to remember that this is not a competition. We are all on our own journey with Christ, who in His infinite wisdom provides a lifetime of growth experiences. It is also important to realize that we cannot do this on our own. We cannot grow toward maximum faith without the help of the Holy Spirit and the other people God has put in our paths to help. And we cannot bear spiritual fruit unless we continue to position our beliefs and actions in line with Christ.

Read John 15:1-11. What does it mean to you to "abide" in Christ? ______________________

____

____

____

In what ways have your relationships changed since deciding to follow Christ? ________

____

____

____

As you focus on areas of alignment, it is quite possible you may be feeling some tension and wrestling with thoughts of where you are falling short, much like a girl who danced flawlessly for 15 minutes in a recent recital. At the end and with tears in her eyes, she hung her head, feeling like a failure and wanting to quit. She wasn't thinking about how she did well most of the time; she was devastated by the few times she got out of step from the others. When she was helped to spend some time looking at her strengths instead of the weaknesses, she was encouraged to work harder and look forward to learning new skills. That is our hope with this chapter: that you will have been inspired and encouraged to continue in your pursuit of God's view of the world.

Now that you have celebrated your alignment with the ways you see God and His world, you will turn next week to areas of misalignment. The next session will provide another opportunity to grow into greater alignment with Him.

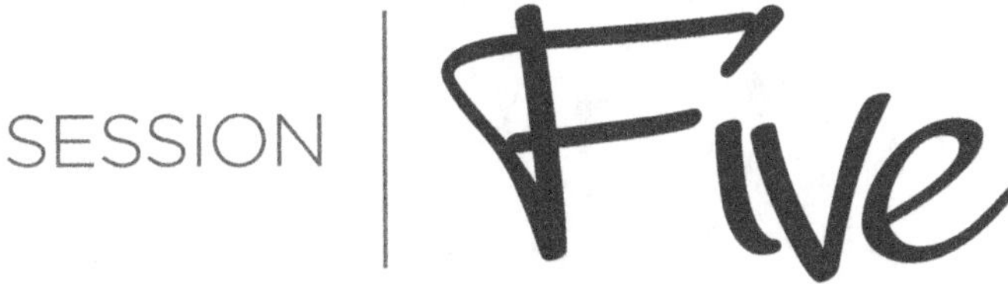

SESSION **Five**

Where You Differ from a

Biblical Worldview –

Growth Areas

Where You Differ from a Biblical Worldview – Growth Areas

In the last session, we celebrated God's goodness in sharing Himself with us, that we were created to know Him and to find our greatest joy in relationship with Him. We also looked at ways that, through His grace, our thinking and beliefs align with the Bible. In this session, though, we will explore the ways your thinking and your life may not align with His view as taught in the Bible.

Now, please don't let this scare you. Everyone is on the Journey toward seeing God more in line with what He has revealed in the Bible. We are in good company when we deal with an area where we need to grow in our knowledge and faith. Growth has been necessary in every generation, beginning with the very first Christians. The author of the Book of Hebrews was challenging the early Jewish Christians to grow.

"For though by this time you ought to be teachers, you need someone to teach you again the basic principles of the oracles of God. You need milk, not solid food, for everyone who lives on milk is unskilled in the word of righteousness, since he is a child. But solid food is for the mature, for those who have their powers of discernment trained by constant practice to distinguish good from evil." (Hebrews 5:12-14)

Imagine you were one of the intended recipients of this text. What do you think you would have felt? Guilt and embarrassment? Something else? _______________

____

____

____

What do you think milk and solid food represents in the spiritual life of believers? ___

____

____

Let's identify your growth areas. Reviewing the results from your worldview assessment, recording each area on the table below where your view of the world and way of living is misaligned or differs from the biblical worldview categories.

Category	Topics	Areas of Misalignment (Indicate modules where the assessment identifies that you possess something other than a biblical worldview)
1	**Bible, Truth, and Morals**	
2	**Faith Practices**	
3	**God, Creation, and History**	
4	**Lifestyle, Behavior, and Relationships**	
5	**Sin, Salvation, and the God Relationship**	
6	**Family, Value of Life, Human Character & Nature, and Purpose & Calling**	

Let's take a moment to consider **the ways you differ** from the biblical worldview. For each module other than Biblical Worldview that you have identified, refer to the description provided in your assessment results or to Appendix D in this workbook to learn more about that competing worldview by considering the following questions:

What is your overall reaction to how you differ from a biblical worldview? ____________

____

____

Were there areas of difference that surprised you? Why? ________________________

____

____

Can you recall how you came to your views of the world that differ from the Bible?

____

____

____

How Our Worldview Gets Distorted

When it comes to beliefs about God, some false, inaccurate, and distorted beliefs often get mixed in with biblical beliefs. This happens in much the same way as weeds begin to grow in your garden. Most of our beliefs about God develop from our relationship with family and friends. We are also exposed to a variety of beliefs and ideas through such venues as TV, film, and social media. These situations can all be sources of misbeliefs. Do you remember the game Telephone from childhood? In this game, everyone sits in a circle and one person whispers a sentence to the person next to them. That person then whispers the sentence to the next one, and so on until the last person has heard the message. That person speaks out loud what he or she heard and usually a ton of laughter erupts because it got completely messed up and doesn't make sense at all. Now, if the person at the beginning had written their sentence on a piece of paper that was passed from one to the next, then all the participants would have had the exact same information conveyed—although, admittedly it wouldn't be quite as much fun. But from this childhood game we can see how important it is to go to God's written word to check and see if our learned beliefs and understanding is Biblical or if we have started accepting some aspects of one of the competing worldviews.

We can trust the Bible to be accurate because we know that the original Scriptures were painstakingly copied by scribes to ensure accuracy of the text. New Testament letters were copied and carried from place to place where they were often read out loud to groups of believers. More recent translations, such as the ESV, have worked from the original writings in Hebrew and Greek instead of interpreting from other translations.

Blatantly false or inaccurate beliefs are easier to identify and challenge by comparing them with Scripture itself. Distorted beliefs can be more difficult to see because they may appear right or true at the surface, but as we look closely we see aspects of untruth. They usually start with some part of the belief that is true, creating the illusion that the whole thing is true. Distorted beliefs may go something like: "But God wants me to be happy." Is it true that God would like His Creation to be happy, or even joyful? Yes, but if we look at Scripture we see that God is less concerned about our present happiness and more concerned with the condition of our soul, as well as our relationship with Him and others. God desires a more complete joy for us that doesn't come from situational pleasures.

How would you explain the difference between happiness and joy? _______________

____

____

____

Can you describe a time you felt joy despite life's difficulties? _______________

____

____

____

____

Another distorted belief looks a lot like legalism. Legalistic beliefs focus on the actions or behaviors Scripture says we should or shouldn't do. It ignores what Scripture says about addressing deeper spiritual needs and getting our hearts in a right relationship with God. Legalism can leave us thinking our relationship with God depends on good behavior. It can seem like checking all the boxes and still feeling empty on the inside, Much like Jesus called the legalistic religious leaders He encountered "whitewashed tombs," meaning they were clean and pure on the outside but dead on the inside. He wasn't saying their good behaviors were bad, just that we should work on getting our inner life right with God and then our actions will flow from that relationship, not the other way around. Sometimes legalism manifests itself in thinking that we must act or look a certain way to be accepted by those who seem to know more than us.

Have you ever found yourself focusing on the way you look or sound to others instead of admitting you don't have it all together? If so, share an example: ________________

____

____

One way false or distorted beliefs creep into our worldview is through the dangerous practice of **trying to understand God and the Bible through the worldview of culture**, rather than striving to understand our culture through a biblical worldview. When we get this mixed up, we run the risk of invalidating or dismissing parts of Scripture that do not line up with our cultural views. We may not do this intentionally, but when cultural views differ from what we are reading in Scripture, there is an uncomfortable tension that arises and won't go away until we find some way to resolve the issue. Our choices are often simple. Either we believe the culture is right, or we believe the Bible is right.

As straightforward as that may seem in theory, in practice it can be complicated. Sometimes we don't see things that clearly fall outside culturally influenced ideals. Take, for example, the story of the man with the withered hand from Mark 3:1-6. Old Testament law forbade working on Sabbath and the religious culture of the time took this to a legalistic extreme. When Jesus came into the synagogue one day and encountered a man with a withered hand, the religious leaders watched to see what He would do so they could catch Him breaking the law. They weren't disappointed. When Jesus told the man to stretch out his hand, it was immediately restored. Instead of being excited at the possibility of seeing a genuine miracle in their presence and being open to the possibility that Jesus was the Messiah they had been longing for, they began looking for ways to destroy Him. Their worldview influenced the way they perceived what was right in front of them. Their belief meant that Jesus could not be the Messiah; He was a lawbreaker. Even though their own law did allow for someone to rescue a cow from a pit, they could not feel the compassion that Jesus felt for this man or see the irony in their situation.

We would like to believe that we would be among the "great crowd" that followed Jesus as He left the synagogue that day instead of with the Pharisees. But if this happened in our day, it is quite likely Jesus would have had a much smaller following. Our culture is becoming more and more skeptical every day, even contemptuous and scornful of things that do not fit its beliefs. It is more important than ever that we strive to see our culture through a biblical worldview.

What are some ways you have wrestled with the tension between biblical and cultural values? ____

____

____

Competing Worldviews That Distort

What a lot of Christians may not be aware of is how easily competing philosophies and worldviews can enter in and distort our understanding of a biblical view of the world. It's like if you were planting a garden and accidentally mixed in a few seeds from an invasive weed variety along with the good seed. Often you can't tell until the plants are nearly fully grown and taking over your garden that they are not producing the results you wanted. In much the same way, individual ideas stemming from present-day worldviews such as Eastern Mysticism, Marxism, Nihilism, Postmodernism, Secular Humanism, Moralistic Therapeutic Deism, and Syncretism are seeping into our lives. It has become such a problem today that it is quite likely nearly everyone reading this has inadvertently accepted some non-biblical beliefs into their own personal worldview.

Read through the brief introductions to some of the most widespread and common worldviews that differ from the Bible in Appendix D near the end of this workbook. They are good examples of how our understanding of the true God of the Bible can become distorted.

If your assessment identifies that you hold any of the competing worldviews, it may help to spend some time understanding the differences between it and the biblical worldview. In that case, consider the following questions:

Which competing worldview have you identified most with now or in the past? (refer to Appendix D as needed)

- ☐ Eastern Mysticism
- ☐ Marxism
- ☐ Nihilism
- ☐ Postmodernism
- ☐ Secular Humanism
- ☐ Moralistic Therapeutic Deism
- ☐ Syncretism
- ☐ Other: ____

Worldviews are not born; they are learned or caught. How did you come to believe the worldview(s) you checked above? _______________________________________

____

____

____

Have you compared any of those competing worldviews with Scripture? ___________

____

____

If so, how does Scripture differ from them? _______________________________

____

____

Syncretism is a blending of several competing worldviews with some biblical ideas
or truths. Are there ways that you can see this happening in your own belief system?
☐ Yes   ☐ No

If so, how or where? ____

____

____

____

In what ways has your worldview affected how you have seen and related to the God
of the Bible? ____

____

____

____

____

As you study competing worldviews, do you see how the biblical worldview is unique
from every other? The biblical worldview teaches us that we were born with a sinful
nature. Our sinful nature inclines us to believe the world revolves around us, and that
we are in control. From infancy, we defined reality in a way that gave us authority
over our own lives. As infants, we were the center of our world. We ran the show.
When we cried, the grown people jumped in to ease our discomfort. This is survival
for babies. But the biblical worldview also says we are not to remain as infants. We
are to see the God of the universe as the ultimate authority over our lives.

Every non-biblical worldview is built on the same sinful, self-focused foundation.
They all teach that we are indeed in control, that we construct our own reality, and
we define truth for ourselves. That is the lie that Adam and Eve bought into: that
they could be gods. The biblical worldview flips our self-centeredness upside down. It

leads us to surrender ourselves to another, to God. But we are constantly falling back into self-centered thoughts, beliefs, and actions. Maturing in faith means constantly working to die to self and live for Christ.

In what ways do you struggle with a self-centered life? __________________________

____

____

____

____

In what ways do you find it easier to surrender to God? ____________________________

____

____

____

____

This session has focused on areas where you are misaligned compared to a biblical worldview. Keep in mind that misalignment identifies areas of potential growth, and this next session will provide opportunity to grow in alignment and joy through knowing God better.

SESSION | *Six*

Building a More Biblical Worldview

Building a More Biblical Worldview

In the previous two sessions, you have explored the ways in which your current worldview aligns or differs from a biblical worldview. Throughout all sessions, we have emphasized the importance of understanding that your worldview is how you not only see the world, but how you see God. We have also emphasized the importance of the Bible in knowing God and how He sees the world.

Surely, changes in your worldview are, in part, changes in your thinking. For example, your past worldview may lead you to think that people exist to make you happy. As you encounter God's view of people, that people are made by God in His image, you have a choice to adopt His way of thinking. You may decide that you are now going to strive to act according to this new belief or worldview. This would be a good thing.

The challenge, however, is that real change involves more than forming a new construct in your mind. It necessitates a supernatural change in heart, and one that only God can do through your faith in Jesus Christ. So, you must change your mind to align with God's view of the world and you must trust, seek, and surrender to God in changing your heart to be able to truly understand and act in accordance with this new worldview.

In this session, we want to help you take a step toward a more biblical worldview. Perhaps you started this process feeling like you already had a biblical worldview. In that case, we want to encourage you in the ways your worldview lines up biblically and challenge you to see this as an opportunity to continue growing. We hope you are feeling anticipation about more fully engaging with the God of the universe and seeing the world as He does! There is truly nothing more soul satisfying than knowing God more intimately and seeing His world more clearly.

A well-established and accepted Christian teaching says, "The chief end of man is to glorify God and enjoy Him forever." To both glorify and enjoy Him; you must know Him. And the better you know Him, the more glory you can give Him and the more joy you can experience in your life. Consider the following practices as foundational in terms of things you do to grow and shape your biblical worldview.

Read the Bible

The best way to start making sure you are moving toward an accurate biblical worldview is to be regularly spending quality time reading the Bible. It's not enough to read passages in a disconnected way, but increased understanding comes when you develop and carry out a systematic plan to eventually get through the Bible in its entirety. Then, when you are done, go back and read it again and again and again. Each time, you will undoubtably gain more knowledge, wisdom, and understanding.

Be honest with yourself and your coach: where are you right now? (check all that apply)

❑ I don't own a Bible.

❑ I'm not sure I believe the Bible is true.

❑ My understanding of the Bible has come mostly from Sunday school, sermons, and/or other people.

❑ My understanding of the Bible has come mostly from TV, movies, and/or social media.

❑ I've tried reading my Bible, but I couldn't understand it.

❑ I read my Bible mostly when I am struggling with a problem in life.

❑ I read my Bible occasionally (1-3 times a month).

❑ I read my Bible frequently (1-3 times a week).

❑ I read my Bible daily (1-3 times a day).

❑ I have read through the entire Bible at least once.

❑ When I read something I don't understand in the Bible, I consult a friend or use a biblical resource to help gain clarity.

❑ I consult my Bible when making major decisions.

❑ Other: ____

This can seem like a daunting task, but it is doable. Here are some helpful suggestions:

- When you sit down to read, pray for the wisdom of God's Holy Spirit to help you understand what you are reading.

- If you need a good study Bible or Bible commentary, investing in one could provide so many additional insights. (See Appendix E for information and suggestions.)

- Consider joining a Bible study group. The insights you gain from one another can be life-changing.

- Sign up to take a Bible class from a local or online Christian college.

- Reach out to a pastor or mature Christian friend with questions or struggles you may be having as you read.

Your word is a lamp to my feet and a light to my path.

Psalm 119:105

Can you identify any growth areas in the way you read and study the Bible, God's Word? If yes, what? ____

Reach Out to Others

It can help to ask others to pray for you, just as the people of Colossae had Paul praying for their spiritual growth (Colossians 1:9-12). Getting others involved also provides accountability to us, knowing that others are praying for us in this way.

It can also help to ask others to study the Bible with you, but it doesn't just help you. When two people study together, both have an opportunity to grow in understanding and wisdom. You can also invite someone to go to a service with you. In addition to worshiping together and hearing messages from skilled Bible teachers, when you initiate a discussion about the message, it helps each of you remember the key points better.

One of the things we must realize is that our beliefs tend to become like the people we spend the most time around. The alcoholic, for instance, spends so much time with other drinkers that he/she has a hard time believing that they have a problem with alcohol. To him or her, "Everyone drinks, and I don't drink any more or less than anyone else."

Think of the people you choose to spend time with. In what ways does your worldview influence them? ____

____

____

____

In what ways does their worldview influence yours? _______________________________

____

____

____

What percentage of your friendships include people who speak positively into your faith and life choices? _______%

Prayer and Meditation

Praying is simply talking to God. When we talk to someone, we begin to build a relationship with them. Prayer is essential if we want to grow spiritually and toward a biblical worldview. If we only talked to our family members a few seconds before meals, our relationship with them would be nearly nonexistent.

Prayer is also about slowing down, being silent, and meditating on God's Word. Meditating includes trying to apply the biblical passages you are reading to your life. Asking yourself, "How does this truth affect what I am thinking and feeling?"

One of the ways God speaks is through helping us recall a specific Bible verse that applies to a situation in our lives. Another way is for His Spirit to communicate a sense of calmness or a sense of uneasiness about a decision we are trying to make. God also speaks sometimes through other believers, friends, or family members that we confide in.

Where are you currently? (check all that apply)

- ☐ I don't know how to pray. (What do I say? Do I sit or kneel?)
- ☐ I don't know how to meditate on Scripture.
- ☐ I intend to pray, but life is busy and I often forget.
- ☐ I pray mainly at mealtime.
- ☐ I pray sometimes silently.
- ☐ I don't feel comfortable praying around or with others.
- ☐ I pray once or twice a week.
- ☐ I pray once or twice a day.
- ☐ My prayers are primarily asking God for something important to me.
- ☐ I pray for friends and family needs.
- ☐ I pray for the needs of people in other places and countries.
- ☐ I say prayers of gratitude and praise often.
- ☐ My prayer life has grown as I've learned more about God.
- ☐ I think of God as "Abba Father" (Daddy) when I pray.
- ☐ Other: ____

Find Out More about Yourself

One way to learn more about God is to understand yourself better. One of the great historical figures in Christian history, St. Augustine, wrote, "Grant, Lord, that I may know myself that I might know Thee." You were created to reflect God's image, so learning how He put you together can help you understand some of His characteristics.

For instance, when we are creative, we reflect God the Creator. When we have a sense of right and wrong, justice and value, we resemble God's perfect justice. When we reason and strive to make sense of things, we look a little like our heavenly father who is orderly and just. He made us to experience an incredibly wide range of emotions, including how to feel love for one another. We have the ability to weep as Jesus did near Lazarus' tomb. In so many ways, we have the ability to reflect the glory of our Father in Heaven.

Consider the following questions: If you have completed the *Starting the Journey* series, you may want to refer back to some of your answers.

Our greatest growth often comes from expanding our strengths. What things, people, or routines might contribute to the development of a more biblical worldview? _____

____

____

Competing worldviews have a way of seeping into our beliefs in God and a right relationship with Him. What is one thing you might do to make changes from misalignment toward a more biblical worldview? __________________________________

____

Obstacles to Change

An obstacle is something that gets in the way of reaching where you want to go. If you want to know God better, which includes knowing how He sees you and the world, then you will need to deal with the things that get in your way. So, consider the following questions:

What are your obstacles to moving toward a more biblical worldview? _____________

____

____

Considering one of your regular days, what activities or things are most valuable to you that might actually be becoming obstacles for real growth? (You might consider how you spend your time and/or money to answer this question.) _______________

____

Have any competing worldviews caused any obstacles in your spiritual growth? ____

____

____

What is it about the obstacle that is enticing you to choose it over God? __________

____

____

What else might hinder you in making time to know God better? ________________

____

____

Consider the following as you develop a more biblical worldview:

"See to it that no one takes you captive by philosophy and empty deceit, according to human tradition, according to the elemental spirits of the world, and not according to Christ." (Colossians 2:8)

In Jesus' Parable of the Sower, as written in Luke 8:5-15, we see that the cares of this world and the riches or pleasures of life can prevent or hinder spiritual growth. What that means for us is that we may learn a particular truth about God's view of the world, but before it has a chance to sink in and change how we believe and act, the distractions and the cynical nature of this world get in the way choking it out.

Read the passage in Luke 8:5-15. What does Jesus' say the seed represents in this parable? (hint: verse 11) ____

____

Can you relate to the parable at all?   ☐ Yes   ☐ No   If so, how? If not, why not? ____

____

____

If we want to bear good fruit, we should surrender to the power of the Holy Spirit who is the One who cultivates those qualities in our lives. The Spirit brings our faith in Christ to life, and continuously focusing on Christ will produce fruit.

"For this very reason, make every effort to supplement your faith with virtue, and virtue with knowledge, and knowledge with self-control, and self-control with steadfastness, and steadfastness with godliness, and godliness with brotherly affection, and brotherly affection with love. For if these qualities are yours and are increasing, they keep you from being ineffective or unfruitful in the knowledge of our Lord Jesus Christ." (2 Peter 1:5-8).

Considering the above verses, what might it look like to apply them in moving toward a more biblical worldview? _______________________________________

____

____

Now that you've begun the process of building a more biblical worldview, the next session will help you create objective and practical next steps toward that end.

SESSION **Seven**

Setting Goals toward a More Biblical Worldview

Setting Goals toward a More Biblical Worldview

It can be very easy to assume that because you have been thinking, reading, and talking about a biblical worldview, change has taken or is taking place. Change, however, requires more than new information. No matter how strongly you reject old information or accept the new, it is essential to make a specific plan. This plan can then become your pathway toward seeing real change. In this session we will begin working on your plan by creating some goals.

Once you have goals in mind, you and your coach can create some action steps that lead toward attaining your goals. This session is devoted to helping you determine those goals and action steps on your journey toward maximum faith.

Here is a list of the "Top 10" most prevalent "Seductive Unbiblical Ideas" embraced by American adults *according to recent research using the American Worldview Inventory 2021, by Dr. George Barna, Director of Research at the Arizona Christian University's Cultural Research Center.* Check the ideas you can recognize in your own worldview beliefs now, or in the past, that have gotten in the way:

- ❑ The spiritually inclusive idea that "having faith matters more than what faith you have"
- ❑ All faiths are of equal value.
- ❑ Belief in "karma," the idea rooted in Eastern religions that "you get what you give"
- ❑ The dismissal of absolute truth
- ❑ Commitment to personal, subjective morality
- ❑ The idea that people are "basically good"
- ❑ Success is determined by happiness, comfort, goodness, or fulfilled potential.
- ❑ Sexual relations apart from marriage are morally acceptable.
- ❑ Rejection of the notion that people are inherently sinful
- ❑ The conclusion that the purpose of accumulated personal wealth is unrelated to God's purposes

If your worldview has any of these or other competing beliefs in it, such as Syncretism, now would be a good time to explore goal setting toward change. One way to do that is to identify the specific things you believe and then research what the Bible says about those things.

Your Personal Worldview

In Session 2, you had the opportunity to identify your beliefs and actions, that were current at the time, based on each of the six Arizona Christian University Worldview Assessment categories. In this session, we will look at the same categories from the perspective of God's Word. In each section you will see suggested Bible verses to read and reflect on. Make notes about what you learn about the biblical worldview related to each category.

Category #1: Bible, Truth, and Morals

This category examines what you believe about the Bible and how it affects your behavior, your perspectives on the concept and pursuit of truth, and your ideas about discerning right and wrong (i.e., morality), and what that looks like in practice.

Read the following passages from Scripture:

Bible	Truth	Morals
• 2 Peter 1:20-21	• John 8:32	• Matthew 7:12
• 2 Timothy 3:14-16	• John 16:13	• Romans 13:8-10
• Hebrews 4:12	• John 17:17	• Mark 7:20-23
• John 1:14.	• John 4:24	• Romans 12:2

Write down what Scripture says about this category: Bible, Truth, Morals: _________

____

____

Growth areas: (Where do you need to grow more in this category regarding beliefs and/or actions?) ____

____

If this Scripture reflection has impacted your understanding, how might that be reflected in the way you live out God's truths and moral standards? _______________

____

____

____

Category #2: Faith Practices

This includes beliefs and activity related to evangelism, worship, prayer, confession, and spiritual growth, and how you handle purpose, temptation, and sin.

Many who first profess belief in Jesus simply stop there. They believe they are going to heaven so there is no need for further growth. But Scripture says we are to not stay as baby Christians but instead continue to grow and mature. Faith can be compared to physical strength and the importance of training our bodies to do what we need them to do.

Read the following passages from Scripture:

- Philippians 1:9-11

- 1 Timothy 4:7-8

- 1 Peter 3:15

- Ephesians 4:11-16

- Acts 1:8

- Romans 12:2

Write down what Scripture says about this category: Faith Practices: _______________

____

____

Growth areas: (Where do you need to grow more in this category regarding beliefs and/or actions?) ____

____

If this Scripture reflection has impacted your understanding of your faith practices, how might that be reflected in the way you live? _______________________________

____

____

____

Category #3: God, Creation, and History

This section explores what you believe about the existence, nature, and work of the God of Israel, the Trinity, Satan, and the meaning of world history.

Read the following passages from Scripture:

- Isaiah 48:12-13

- Genesis 1:1, 26

- Romans 11:33-36

- 2 Corinthians 3:17

- John 14:10

- Proverbs 31:8-9

Write down what Scripture says about this category: God, creation and history: _____

____

____

Growth areas: (Where do you need to grow more in this category regarding beliefs and/or actions?) ____

____

If your understanding of God, Creation, and history were to change, how would it impact the way you live each day? ____

____

____

____

Category #4: Lifestyle, Behavior, and Relationships

This module of questions explored your perspectives related to your lifestyle activities and preferences, how you interact with resources and opportunities, and the nature and goal of your interpersonal relationships.

Read the following passages from Scripture:

- Proverbs 16:3, 9; 15:22; 19:21

- Jeremiah 29:11

- Philippians 4:6

- James 4:13-15

- Luke 12:15

- 1 Timothy 6:17-19

Write down what Scripture says about this category: Lifestyle, Behavior, and Relationships: ____

____

____

Growth areas: (Where do you need to grow more in this category regarding beliefs and/or actions?) ____

____

If you were to think differently about this category, what would change? How would it impact your lifestyle? How would it impact your relationships? ______________

____

____

____

____

____

Category #5: Sin, Salvation, and the God Relationship

This module included questions regarding how you think about and address sin; your beliefs and choices related to personal salvation; and the nature and pursuit of your relationship with God.

Read the following passages from Scripture:

- James 4:17

- Romans 3:23

- 1 Corinthians 10:13

- 2 Corinthians 6:18

- Galatians 4:5-7

Write down what Scripture says about this category: Sin, Salvation, and the God Relationship: ____

____

____

____

____

Growth areas: (Where do you need to grow more in this category regarding beliefs and/or actions?) ____

____

____

Putting this into practical terms, what might be different in your life, actions and relationships if you are able to better align your beliefs in this category with Scripture?

____

____

____

____

____

Category #6: Family, Value of Life, Human Character & Nature, Purpose & Calling

A series of crucial worldview factors that are not reported individually but as a group of factors. This includes perspectives about marriage, children, and family, as well as the value and dignity of life. Also includes the purpose and calling for each human being, and the nature and character components of every individual. These areas are part of a person's overall worldview. The biblical worldview perspective for understanding these factors is found in Scripture.

Read the following passages from Scripture:

- Genesis 1:26-27

- Jeremiah 1:5

- Galatians 5:22-23

- Luke 10:25-37

- Ephesians 4:11-16

- 1 Corinthians 6:19-20

- Romans 5:3-5

Write down what Scripture says about this category: Family, Value of Life, Human Character & Nature, Purpose & Calling: _______________________________________

____

____

____

____

Growth areas: (Where do you need to grow more in this category regarding beliefs and/or actions?) ____

____

____

____

If your worldview grew to reflect God's view of the world more, how would that translate into the way you make decisions at work or school? Would you vote differently? ____

____

____

Before we move on to making your change list, let's look again at the seven cornerstones of a biblical worldview that were introduced in Session 2. Read through this list and identify the ones you are struggling with in either beliefs or actions:

- ❏ 1. An orthodox, biblical understanding of God
- ❏ 2. All human beings are sinful by nature; every choice we make has moral contours and consequences.
- ❏ 3. Jesus Christ is the sole means to individual salvation, accomplished through our acknowledgment and confession of our sins and complete reliance on His grace for the forgiveness of those sins.
- ❏ 4. The entire Bible is true, reliable and relevant, making it the best moral guide for every person, in all situations.
- ❏ 5. Absolute moral truth exists—and those truths are defined by God, described in the Bible, and unchanging across time and cultures.
- ❏ 6. The ultimate purpose of human life is to know, love, and serve God with all your heart, mind, strength, and soul.
- ❏ 7. Success on Earth is best understood as consistent obedience to God—in thoughts, words, and actions.

You may be wondering why we spend so much time emphasizing the importance of how our actions follow our beliefs. It might be helpful to look at some examples.

Wess Stafford, former CEO of Compassion International, once was overheard to have said, "No one cares how much you know until they know how much you care." There is so much wisdom in that statement. Our actions speak louder than our words and communicate to others our true underlying beliefs. A person is thought to have integrity when their words and actions, which demonstrate beliefs and behaviors, match.

Let's look at the story of Frank Camp. You probably have never heard of him. Frank was not a public figure, and he wasn't known nationally or internationally. Except for a brief stint in the navy, Frank lived in only two different counties in the state of Iowa. But he was loved and respected by nearly all who knew him. Frank loved the Lord and served Him faithfully, even when asked to do things that were outside his comfort level. He taught his kids to treat others with respect because they were also children of God. He quietly visited family members in prison and the hospital. He gave generously to needs without fanfare, knowing that his reward would be in Heaven. With a gentle spirit, Frank led his family, showing integrity and honor. To this day, his children and grandchildren are teaching the next generation about their great-grandfather's faith, love, and character.

Most of us will never be a Wess Stafford in charge of an international ministry. But we can all be like Frank. Think about where God has put you today and whom you can influence for Him.

Your Change List

Congratulations, you have made it through some of the toughest parts of this journey! Personal exploration can be hard and tiring. But now you have come to the place where can act on what you have learned. You can begin to plan for change. Let's start by identifying some things you would like to change regarding your worldview.

Look at the notes you've made in this journey so far, especially in the areas where you identified ways your worldview is different from the biblical worldview. What are the top five areas you now have a desire to change? Prioritize them below. When arranging them, consider several factors:

- Are any areas easer to start with than others? Sometimes starting with an easy task produces quicker results that increase our confidence level and motivation to keep going.

- Are any more urgent than others? If there is a change that is causing some difficulty in your life, it might be good to start there. For instance, if an important relationship is causing a lot of stress in your life, working on resolution could free up mental and emotional energy to work on other things.

- Do any areas require another change to take place first? If one goal is that you want to spend more time reading God's Word, you must first figure out how to find the time. One goal might be to consider activities that you could eliminate to make more time for God's Word.

1. ____

2. ____

3. ____

4. ____

5. ____

Goal Setting

Now as you set goals, consider the acronym S.M.A.R.T. Goals often succeed or fail before they leave the starting gate. One way to give yourself a good start is to make sure your goals are stated in a way that addresses the five S.M.A.R.T. rules below:

Specific – Make sure your goals are not vague, general, or easy to misinterpret.

Measurable – How are you going to track your progress?

Attainable – Are they realistic and within reach?

Relevant – Does this goal relate directly to the issue you are trying to address?

Time Bound – Select a realistic completion or reassess date.

We also recommend trying to accomplish only one goal at a time. Once you have gained success in that goal, you will undoubtably feel encouraged to tackle the next one.

Let's practice a bit. For instance, if your desire is to read your Bible more, that would be a good objective, but wouldn't serve as a helpful goal. As written, there would be no way to know if you have been successful because it isn't specific or measurable, nor does it have a realistic target date.

Instead, consider something like this: "I'm going to set my alarm for 15 minutes earlier than usual each workday for the next two weeks. When I get up, I will pour myself a cup of coffee and read my Bible for 10 minutes, starting with the first chapter of John." This goal would be very specific, measurable, relevant, and time bound. You would then have to ask yourself if it is attainable. Can you really get up 15 minutes earlier? If not, consider picking a time of day that would be more realistic for you.

Now it is your turn. Look at your change list above. Take your first goal and work it out below in the following exercise. You can repeat this process for each of the additional goals you identified.

State your overall objective (what you want to accomplish): _________________

____

____

Define your **SMART** goal (how you want to accomplish your objective):

Be **Specific** about what you are going to attempt to do. _________________

____

____

____

How are you going to **Measure** your progress? _________________________

____

____

____

How do you know it is **Attainable**? ___________________________________

____

____

____

How will this goal be **Relevant** to your overall objective? _______________

____

____

____

How much **Time** must pass before you know if you have been successful? _______

____

____

____

Remember, the goal itself should be a next step toward a more biblical worldview. You are simply planning one step at a time. Here are some suggestions for possible goals. If you are still stuck coming up with an idea, you can choose to adopt one or more of the ideas below and turn them into **SMART** goals for yourself:

- Read the Bible for five to 15 minutes every day.

- Find a friend or small group to pray for you and hold you accountable.

- Take a prayer walk with God three times a week.

- Reduce your screen time by _______ minutes a week and replace it with _______________.

- Memorize _______ Bible verses related to a particular worldview belief you are trying to change.

- Find a church (if not already connected).

- Attend church more often or get more involved.

Meet with a pastor or church leader to discuss an area of growth and see if there is any way they can help.

Do further research on an area of growth that leads to better understanding of the importance of knowing and living out the biblical worldview.

What is the first **SMART** goal that you will begin this week? _________________

____

____

In your next and final session of this series, you will share your experiences working out your first **SMART** goal and explore successes and/or failures you encountered along the way.

Talk with your coach now to determine the date for your follow-up Session 8, giving yourself adequate time to make some progress on the goal you select for growth.

Session 8 date: _____ / _____ / _____

Time: _____ : _____ am/pm

"Therefore, as you received Christ Jesus the Lord, so walk in Him, rooted and built up in Him and established in the faith, just as you were taught, abounding in thanksgiving." (Colossians 2:6-7)

SESSION | # Eight

Follow-Up Support and Encouragement

Follow-Up, Support, and Encouragement

Hopefully you have had the opportunity to begin working on at least one of the goals you identified in the last session. How is it going? Change is often difficult. Setting out to change a habit, either starting a new one or breaking an old one, will be uncomfortable until you do it long enough to settle into a new "normal." Often this takes at least six or more weeks of intentionally pushing yourself to do what you eventually want to become a new habit in your life.

So, how did you do?

What goal(s) did you achieve? ____

____

How? ____

____

What goal(s) did you make some progress on? _________________________________

____

How? ____

____

What goals are still in the future? ____

____

____

Why are they important? ____

____

What goals would you revise or eliminate? ___________________________________

____

Why? ____

____

Working through Resistance

If you haven't seemed to make much progress toward your goal(s), consider what may be causing some resistance. Resistance can come from outside or inside forces. Have a conversation with your coach and maybe the two of you can come up with some insights or ideas. Often, we learn more from identifying the source(s) of resistance than we do from our successes. Consider the following example in the story below.

Ellie decided that reading her Bible more regularly would be a good first step toward growing a more Biblical worldview. She needed to find a way to better understand what she was reading in her Bible. She thought maybe a study group would be a good option. With her coach, Ellie set the following SMART goal: "I am going to reach out to my church by phone or email early this week and ask for recommendations of study groups that meet in my area during the evenings when I am off work. I will then contact two or three of them by the end of the week to select one that I want to attend."

During the next session, Ellie admitted to her coach that she hadn't made the progress she had hoped for. Together they explored what got in the way. Ellie said she didn't have any trouble contacting the church and they sent her a list of study groups in her area complete with meeting dates and times. But that's where the progress ended. Every time Ellie considered the list, she seemed to feel more and more uncomfortable.

As they talked about her feelings, Ellie began to realize her hesitation seemed to be coming from worry that others would know more about the Bible than she did, or that she would be afraid to speak up in the group. Her coach assured her that the study groups were for learning, not demonstrating prior knowledge. She also suggested that when she contacted the group leader, Ellie might share her concerns so they could work out a plan for how she could feel more comfortable in the new group.

With new encouragement to work through her own resistance, Ellie called one of the group leaders and shared her concerns. That woman assured Ellie that everyone feels a little nervous at first and welcomed her to the next group meeting to give it a try.

Can you relate to the woman in this story?   ☐ Yes   ☐ No

If so, were there times you were able to work through the resistance? _____________

____

____

____

Were there other times it stopped you from moving forward? ____________________

____

____

The CRC Assessment:

If you were to retake the worldview assessment now that you have completed *Journey toward Maximum Faith*, do you believe you would answer the questions differently?   ☐ Yes   ☐ No

Please explain your answer above ____

____

____

____

____

Where do I go now?

Options:

1. If this has been a helpful process for you, you might consider coaching others. If your worldview assessment indicated that you have a Biblical worldview, your wisdom and insight can make a difference in the lives of those who struggle in this area. If you have a desire to help others grow, talk with your coach to find out more.

2. Join a small group at your church or consider starting a group in your area. Groups are great ways to continue your spiritual, personal, and relational growth. Ask your coach for more information.

3. Continue meeting with your coach. Have a conversation with your coach about possibly continuing to meet for a specific timeframe. There are many great books and Bible studies available. Keep an eye out for future Journey Coaching series as they become available.

4. Serve others. Our spiritual growth and relationship with God expand when we worship God through serving others.

Want more information?

Check out the Appendixes and Reference pages immediately following this session.

Evaluation

How has this *Journey toward Maximum Faith* experience been for you?

❑ Very helpful in understanding myself and my worldview better

❑ Somewhat helpful

❑ Not helpful at all

Please explain: ____

Do you feel this experience has helped you identify specific growth areas?

❑ Yes

❑ Maybe

❑ No

Please explain: ____

Would you recommend Journey Coaching to others?

❑ Yes

❑ Maybe

❑ No

Please explain: ____

Are there any areas you would like to see a Journey Coaching series explore in the future?

❑ Yes ____

❑ No

Was your experience with your coach a positive one?

❑ Yes

❑ Maybe

❑ No

Please explain: ____

Thank you for your feedback. Please take a photo of this response and email it to Terry@JourneyCoaching.org.

How the Three Segments & 10 Stops Line Up

World Citizen:

Individuals who do not have a biblical worldview and who are nowhere close (82% of the population)

Stop 1: Unaware of sin – These are people who are ignorant of any spiritual war and of their own place within it.

Stop 2: Indifferent to sin – These are people who are aware of the concept of sin, but don't necessarily believe in it or care about it.

Stop 3: Worried about sin – These are the people who are starting to question whether they sin and if that matters in the world; they start to feel uneasy about the "what ifs." These are the World Citizens who have the most potential of becoming Emergent Followers and then Integrated Disciples because they are starting to question both their beliefs and behaviors.

Emergent Follower:

Individuals who do not qualify as having a biblical worldview, but whose worldview is greatly influenced by biblical truth and could conceivably become Integrated Disciples given changes in their beliefs and behaviors (14% of the population)

Stop 4: Forgiven for sin – This is the place of being born again. Emergent Followers might be Christians who are forgiven for their sin, but never go beyond this belief into actual change in their actions or worldview.

Stop 5: Forgiven and active – These Christians may be committed to spiritual growth or a faith community but are not yet at the point of full understanding of what a biblical worldview looks like or requires of them.

Stop 6: Holy discontent – In many cases, this may be the awakening of an Emergent Follower, a call by God to go deeper. They are troubled by the stagnant position of their faith and are starting to come out of the numbness of going through the motions.

Possibly Stop 7: Broken by God – This is a season of growing from an Emergent Follower to an Integrated Disciple. Believers are confronted by their own spiritual state and what more God has for them. People could be on either side of the EF/ID line at this stop.

Integrated Disciple:

Individuals who have integrated their faith into every dimension of their life and live as disciples of Jesus Christ (4% of the population)

Possibly Stop 7: Broken by God – This is a season of growing from an Emergent Follower to an Integrated Disciple. Believers are confronted by their own spiritual state and what more God has for them. People could be on either side of the EF/ID line at this stop.

Stop 8: Surrender and submission – This is the acting out of the lessons in stop 7. It is consciously giving control over to God every day.

Stop 9: Profound love of God – Believers reach a new level of depth and enjoyment in their relationship with God.

Stop 10: Profound love of people – Their love for God spills over into active and otherworldly love for people.

Six Categories

1. Bible, Truth, and Morals

What you believe about the Bible and how it affects your behavior, your perspectives on the concept and pursuit of truth, and your ideas about discerning right and wrong and what it looks like in practice.

2. Faith Practices

How you apply what you believe about the Bible. How you put those perspectives into practice. Includes beliefs and activity related to evangelism, worship, prayer, confession, and spiritual growth; and how you handle purpose, temptation, and sin.

3. God, Creation, and History

What you believe about the existence, nature, and work of the God of Israel, the Trinity, Satan, and the meaning of world history

4. Lifestyle, Behavior, and Relationships

Your perspectives related to your lifestyle activities and preferences, how you interact with resources and opportunities, and the nature and goal of your interpersonal relationships.

5. Sin, Salvation, and the God Relationship

How you think about and address sin, your beliefs and choices related to personal salvation, and the nature and pursuit of your relationship with God.

6. Family, Value of Life, Human Character & Nature, and Purpose & Calling

These make up the sixth category of items included in the overall assessment results. However, you will not see individual category results for them. (For purposes of this resource, Categories 6, 7, and 8 are combined into one category.) A series of crucial worldview factors that are not reported individually but as a group of factors. This includes perspectives about marriage, children, and family, as well as the value and dignity of life. Also includes the purpose and calling for each human being, and the nature and character components of every individual. These areas are part of a person's overall worldview. The biblical worldview perspective for understanding these factors is found in Scripture.

Maximum Faith 10 Stops

- ☐ <u>**Stop 1:**</u> **Ignorance of the concept or existence of sin**

  This is the stop where everybody begins, oblivious to the existence of God or His moral and spiritual standards.

- ☐ <u>**Stop 2:**</u> **Aware of and indifferent to sin**

  At this stop, a person becomes aware of the concept of sin but rejects it as a standard to live by.

- ☐ <u>**Stop 3:**</u> **Concern about the implications of personal sin**

  At this stop, a person begins to embrace the possibility that sin exists and starts to consider its implications for their life and eternity. They may even begin to pursue or attend a church.

- ☐ <u>**Stop 4:**</u> **Confess sins and ask Jesus Christ to be Lord and Savior**

  This stop is where a person confesses himself or herself as a sinner and turns to God for forgiveness in Jesus Christ. For many, their spiritual growth may stall at this point if they believe their prayer for forgiveness is all they need for living the Christian life.

- ☐ <u>**Stop 5:**</u> **Commitment to faith activities**

  At this stop, a person's spiritual hunger compels them to get involved with a church and to begin to engage in that community's faith activities (i.e.: worship services, Christian education classes, personal worship time, and service opportunities).

- ☐ <u>**Stop 6:**</u> **Experience a prolonged period of spiritual discontent**

  This stop is where faith activities turn into a set of lifeless rituals and routines that don't feed a growing relationship with God. A new discontent arises that either leads to retreat into continued lifeless rituals or drives them to pursue something more.

- ☐ <u>**Stop 7:**</u> **Experience personal brokenness**

  This stop brings someone to a state of brokenness over their deep sin of self-reliance. They realize how much they remain in control and turn to God in confession and repentance.

- ☐ <u>**Stop 8:**</u> **Choose to surrender and submit fully to God**

  At this stop a person begins to understand what total surrender, complete submission, and utter dependence on God really mean. They begin to allow God to remake their life by giving Him more and more control.

☐ <u>**Stop 9:**</u> **Enjoy a profound intimacy with and love for God**

This stop is where someone experiences a new deep and profound experience with God and His love. Life takes on new meaning as each day is lived in the presence of God with increasing levels of joy, peace, wisdom, and depth of purpose.

☐ <u>**Stop 10:**</u> **Experience a profound compassion and love for humanity**

This last stop is where a deeper relationship with God allows someone to begin to see people, all people, the way He sees them, to hear them as He hears them, and to love them as He loves them.

Competing Worldviews

Eastern Mysticism (Pantheism, Monism, New Age)

Belief in a universal "one" impersonal spiritual force that exists in the natural world. Pantheism essentially means all or everything is a part of this spiritual force. This belief explains that there is a divine force in every human being. There is no evil and we don't need to seek God, but instead just raise our consciousness to realize our inner deity. Through evolution and spiritual practices such as meditation, breathing exercises, crystals, sprit guides, etc., an individual can grow a closer connection to the universal One. This worldview seems to appeal to the human temptation to want to be like God and further separates us from a deep and personal relationship with the God of the Bible.

Marxism (Neo-Marxism, Critical Race Theory, Social Justice)

Starting as a social justice movement hostile toward capitalism and traditional social relationships such as marriage and religion. Marxism believes that there are no supernatural or spiritual things, only material things. There is no god and religion is the "opiate of the masses." Marxism views religion as oppressive and harmful. Rejecting the biblical view of original sin, Marxists believe people are morally good and cooperative by nature. Remove capitalism and oppressive structures; humans will return to their naturally good state. Ethics are related to those things that advance the interests of the oppressed. What ever hinders that advance is morally bad. Christians unwittingly start to adopt these beliefs when they are made to feel guilty or ashamed that they are not a part of the "oppressed" people groups.

Nihilism

This worldview follows the belief that nothing in the world matters or exists. Life is without meaning, purpose, hope, morality, or value. We are only here for a brief time, so do whatever you can to enjoy this momentary existence. Emotions and thoughts are random chemical reactions and have no real purpose. There is no God, soul, judgment, savior, or life after death. Nihilism beliefs seep into Christianity almost unnoticed at times when we start to doubt that God really exists, that He is powerful, or that He is a loving and kind heavenly Father.

Postmodernism (Subjectivism, Eclecticism)

Postmodernism rejects any possibility of objective truth. Everything is subjective. Your truth is yours and my truth is mine. Ethics and morality are up to each individual. If you try to take your truth and apply it to me, you are being oppressive and intolerant. We can construct or deconstruct our truths at any time. Postmodernists reject the idea of God or unchanging truth. Religious people are tricking themselves into believing there is something bigger than themselves or using it to exploit others and exert power. Postmodernism infiltrates Christianity when we focus on religion instead of our ability to have a personal relationship with God.

Secular Humanism (Naturalism)

This worldview states that there is no God and no supernatural. Humans take the place of God in explaining and understanding the world. We are to lead ethical lives striving for personal fulfillment and aspiring to the greater good. The only things that exist are those things that can be experienced through the five senses. Human feelings, emotions, personality, and spirituality are just chemical reactions in the brain. Things outside the natural universe are social constructs from a time when we hadn't evolved more fully. Religious beliefs are dangerous superstitions limiting our potential. Humanists believe that at death we cease to exist. Morality is determined by culture and human consciousness rather than a standard or natural law, and is focused on human need and interest, taking responsibility for our own destiny. This worldview can seem similar to—but is actually a distortion of—the biblical perspective of treating others with dignity and helping to meet the needs of hurting people. Yet we cannot forget that Humanism at its core is atheistic. The biblical view of the dignity of humans and care for others comes from the fact that men and women are created in His image. We were created to reflect God, not be gods. When we hear of people today "deconstructing" their faith, it is possible they were following a form of

Christian Humanist worldview, realizing that their religion was a construct to begin with rather than deeply rooted in relationship with the God of the Bible.

Moralistic Therapeutic Deism

On the surface, this worldview appears to be biblical. In fact, it is more like a softened and distorted version of Biblical Theism. It takes the parts of a biblical worldview that are easy or positive, while ignoring those that are difficult or require self-denial. The goal of this worldview is to live a happy and good life, then go to Heaven when you die. God is seen as benevolent and desiring our happiness. He meets our needs when in trouble or crisis. If people live good lives and do good works, they will have earned their salvation and enter Heaven for eternity when they die. This worldview downplays the gospel message of Jesus' death for our sins. This version of Christianity can be very popular for those who find the more challenging Bible passages troublesome. It is tempting to create in our minds a God whom we want to believe in, rather than wrestle with understanding the real God who is.

Syncretism

This last category is the most prevalent worldview in America. It is created by individuals choosing preferred principles or beliefs from each of the other popular worldview philosophies and combining them into a custom-built worldview. Syncretism distorts the biblical worldview in much more subtle ways than other competing worldviews because it can incorporate just enough biblical beliefs to feel "Christian." For example: the person who says they believe in Jesus as God's Son, but also that they believe Christianity is only one of many ways to Heaven. George Barna provides this helpful definition:

Basically, a person adopts any belief system that most benefits them in the moment, even if it contradicts what they decided or believed only minutes earlier.

Finding a Bible

Finding a Bible can be confusing and overwhelming unless you are equipped with a basic understanding of the primary differences and types of translations from the original Hebrew and Greek texts.

Major Bible translations typically reflect one of three general philosophies: **formal equivalence, functional equivalence**, and **optimal equivalence**.

Try not to get hung up on the big words. **Formal equivalence translations** can be identified as **word-for-word** translations. These attempt to translate the Bible as literally as possible, keeping the sentence structure and meanings intact if possible. They are more historically and factually accurate than other versions but can also be more difficult to read and understand. A word-for-word translation is attempting to simply translate each word without providing an additional interpretation for you. The NASB and KJV are representatives of this camp.

Functional equivalence translations can be identified as **thought-for-thought** translations. These attempt to translate the text so it has the same effect on the current reader as it had on the ancient reader. They try to keep intact the historical and factual details, while making the ideas easier to read for modern readers. A translation with functional equivalence is translating an entire thought from the Greek text. In a sense, it has begun to interpret the thought for you as it translates it into English. The NLT exemplifies this theory.

Optimal equivalence translations fall somewhere in the middle of the spectrum. They exist between the former two approaches, balancing the tension between accuracy and ease of reading. While striving for precision in translation, they also seek clarity for the modern-day reader. The NIV and TNIV are examples of this translation type.

How to choose?

There are several factors to consider whether you are purchasing a Bible for yourself or someone else. There is no right or wrong choice. Instead, it is a matter of being aware of their differing intentions and being wise about which one or ones would best help you. For those new to reading Scripture, the thought-for-thought translations might be a good choice for a first Bible. They are written in a way that is easier and seems more familiar to other books they might sit down and read.

For those wanting a deeper study of the Bible, word-for-word translations take some concentration, but you will be rewarded with a more intact understanding of the ideas the original writers were attempting to communicate. Really serious students may want an Interlinear Bible. This type has the original Hebrew or Greek words alongside the English equivalent and the Strong's index codes. Strong's is a reference book you can buy that has indexed all the original Hebrew and Greek words, giving students of the Bible an opportunity to compare passages that contain the same words.

Other things to consider when purchasing a Bible are:

1. Is there a specific translation that your church or study group uses? It may be easier to follow along if you have the same translation.
2. Would a Study Bible be helpful? Study Bibles often include helpful extras such as concordances, notes, articles, reading plans, charts, and maps. Study Bibles can be found in each of the main Bible translation types.
3. Are you interested in comparing more than one type of translation as you study? Many people benefit from reading a passage from the thought-for-thought Bible for basic understanding and then read the same passage in the word-for-word Bible for added clarity.
4. You may want to consider starting with reading an online Bible until you figure out which one is best for you. Here are some resources that allow you to read the Bible passages in most English versions. Many of them are free.

- **Bible.com**

- **BibleGateway.com**

- **BibleStudyTools.com**

- **BibleHub.com** – Has the option to read the Bible in different languages in addition to English (Topical, Greek, Hebrew) as well as utilize references such as concordances, commentaries, dictionaries, sermons, and devotionals.

- **BlueLetterBible.com**

- **Biblica.com**

- Many different Bible apps available for phones and tablets

Still having trouble deciding? A helpful resource to learn more as well as purchase a Bible can be found at:

ChristianBook.com/Page/Bibles/About-Bibles/About-Translations

Worldview

Worldview is the filter through which you experience, interpret, and respond to the world; it informs an individual's thinking and decision-making.

Biblical Worldview

The biblical worldview is a means of experiencing, interpreting, and responding to reality in light of a biblical perspective. Having a biblical worldview means "thinking like Jesus, so that you can act like Jesus."

Coaching

"Coaching is the art and practice of enabling individuals and groups to move from where they are to where they want to be. Christian coaching is the art and practice of enabling individuals and groups to move from where they are to where God wants them to be." (Gary R. Collins)

Disciple/Discipleship

Being a Disciple of Jesus.

The Great Commission – Jesus's call to His disciples to "go and make disciples of all peoples," found in Matthew 28:19, emphasizes the importance of being not just a convert to Christianity, but being a disciple of Jesus Christ. You cannot be a genuine convert to the Christian faith without being a disciple of Jesus. Those who have embraced Christ as their savior, perhaps after saying a prayer acknowledging sin and asking for forgiveness, are not necessarily disciples of Jesus. Such individuals are exercising what Dietrich Bonhoeffer labeled "cheap grace"—seeking eternal peace without true repentance.

Jesus was quite clear that being a disciple was not quick, simple, or easy. He described disciples as those who consistently obey His teaching (John 8:31); tangibly love other disciples (John 13:35); produce an abundance of spiritual fruit (John 18:8); live for and love God beyond all else (Luke 14:26), submit to God's authority in all matters (Luke 14:27), and surrender everything to be a devoted follower and servant of Christ (Luke 14:33).

In studying the disciple-making practices of Jesus, it becomes clear that one makes disciples through a close, personal relationship in which the disciple spends a lot of high-quality time living life together and refining one's lifestyle to reflect the life principles modeled by Jesus.

In the end, a disciple of Jesus is someone dedicated to thinking like Jesus so that they can live like Jesus. Those who are able to think like Him and convert their choices into a lifestyle that reflects that of Jesus are His disciples.

Emergent Follower

Segment 2. Individuals who have some aspects of a biblical worldview and may be greatly influenced by biblical truth. These individuals could grow to become integrated disciples assuming changes in their beliefs and behaviors. 14% of the population. (See Appendix A for more information.)

Integrated Disciple

Segment 3. Individuals who have greatly integrated their faith into every dimension of their life and are striving to live as disciples of Jesus Christ through dependence on the Holy Spirit. 4% of the population. (See Appendix A for more information.)

Orthodox

Conforming to what is generally or traditionally accepted as right or true, established and approved. A religious belief or interpretation that was handed down by a church's founders or leaders.

World Citizen

Segment 1. Individuals who do not yet have a discernable biblical worldview. About 82% of the population. (See Appendix A for more information.)

References

Barna, George. "Mapping the Journey." In *Maximum Faith: Live like Jesus, Experience Genuine Transformation*, 15-32. Austin, TX: Fedd and Company, Inc., 2011.

Barna, George. *American Worldview Inventory 2020-21: The Annual Report on the State of Worldview in the United States.* Glendale, AZ: Arizona Christian University Press, 2021.

Carlson, Terry and Mike Calacci. *Starting the Journey: Your Personal Workbook.* Swisher, IA: Journey Press, 2020.

Collins, Gary R. *Christian Coaching: Helping Others Turn Potential into Reality.* Colorado Springs, CO: NavPress, 2009; 23.

Recommended Reading

Packer, J.I. *Knowing God.* Downers Grove, IL: InterVarsity Press, 1993.

Tozer, A.W. *The Pursuit of God: The Human Pursuit for the Devine.* Chicago, IL: Moody Publishers, 2015.

McDowell, Josh and Sean McDowell, Ph.D. *Evidence that Demands a Verdict: Life-Changing Truth for a Skeptical World.* Nashville, TN: Thomas Nelson, Inc., 2017.

Strobel, Lee. *The Case for Christ: A Journalist's Personal Investigation of the Evidence for Jesus.* Grand Rapids, MI: Zondervan, 2016.

Jennings, T.R. *The God-Shaped Brain: How Changing Your View of God Transforms Your Life.* Downers Grove, IL: InterVarsity Press, 2013.

Newberg, Andrew and Mark Robert Waldman. *How God Changes Your Brain: Breakthrough Findings from a Leading Neuroscientist.* New York: Ballantine Books, 2010.

Websites

ChristianBook.com/Page/Bibles/About-Bibles/About-Translations

GotQuestions.org/Bible-God-Word.html

Dr. George Barna, Director of Research. American Worldview Inventory 2021 Release #5: Top 10 Most Seductive Unbiblical Ideas Embraced by Americans. Cultural Research Center Release Date: June 22, 2021. **ArizonaChristian.edu/WP-Content/Uploads/2021/06/CRC_AWVI2021_Release05_Digital_01_20210618.pdf**

National Survey on Drug Use and Health (NSDUH). **Samhsa.gov/Newsroom/Press-Announcements/20230104/Samhsa-Announces-nsduh-Results-Detailing-Mental-Illness-Substance-Use-Levels-2021**

Wetselaar MJ, Nelson LA, Stewart JA, et al. (2019) Review of the Effect of Religion on Anxiety. *Int J Depress Anxiety* 2016. **DOI.org/10.23937/2643-4059/1710016ClinmedJournals.org/Articles/IJDA/International-Journal-of-Depression-and-Anxiety-IJDA-2-016.php**

TERRY CARLSON

Terry Carlson RN, LMHC, CADC

The concept for Journey Coaching came about during a time when I was working on staff of our local church and saw firsthand many of the discipleship challenges that exist today. Our society has become more technologically advanced than ever, and the downside of that is that people are more isolated and relationally disconnected than before. The *Journey* materials were created primarily to equip believers to respond to the relational needs of people, both inside and outside church walls, and to fulfill Jesus' command to go and make disciples. (Matthew 28:19-20)

Terry is a registered nurse and licensed mental health/substance abuse counselor who has been working in a Christian counseling practice for over 10 years. Baptized at the age of 11, she has devoted her life to growing in her relationship with Christ and serving Him by aiding others to do the same. Terry has been married to Jeff Carlson for 45 years, is a mother of three, and a grandmother of 12.

MIKE CALACCI

Lead Pastor in Chicagoland Area

Mike has been serving the local church for the past 35 years. He has spent his entire ministry career seeking to understand and help people grow in their walk with Jesus Christ. His master's degree and Ph.D. work have centered on education, especially in what the Scriptures teach us about Christian growth. He has also spent the past 12 years helping churches and pastors across the nation work through these same questions and concerns. He shares the core belief with the Journey Team that everyone needs someone walking personally with them in order to grow on their journey with Jesus.

DR. GEORGE BARNA

Dr. George Barna is the co-founder and Director of Research at the Cultural Research Center at Arizona Christian University, focusing on worldview assessment and development, and cultural transformation. He is also a professor at the university. Barna serves as the Senior Research Fellow at Family Research Council's Center for Biblical Worldview and a Fellow at the Townsend Institute at Concordia University. He was the founder of the Barna Group (which he sold in 2009), the Barna Institute, the American Culture and Faith Institute, and Metaformation.

Through these entities, he has conducted groundbreaking research on worldview, cultural transformation, ministry applications, spiritual development, and politics. He has provided research and strategy for several hundred parachurch ministries, thousands of Christian churches, the U.S. military, and Fortune 500 companies.

His most recent book, *Raising Spiritual Champions: Nurturing Your Child's Heart, Mind and Soul*, is the 60th book that Barna has authored or co-authored. His books have addressed social and religious trends, worldview, leadership, spiritual development, church dynamics, and cultural transformation. They include *New York Times* and Amazon bestsellers and several award-winning books. His books have been translated into more than a dozen foreign languages. He is a frequent speaker at events throughout the world, having spoken at more than 1,000 events during the course of his career, including events in 14 different countries.

Prior to joining the faculty of Arizona Christian University, Barna taught at several universities and seminaries, served as the teaching pastor of a large, multi-ethnic church, pastored a house church, and helped to start several churches. He has also served as an elder in several congregations. After graduating summa cum laude from Boston College, Barna earned two master's degrees from Rutgers University and received a doctorate from Dallas Baptist University.

Barna and his wife, Nancy, attended high school, college, and graduate school together before marrying in the Princeton University Chapel in 1978. They have three adopted daughters and three grandchildren and currently live on the central California coast and in the Phoenix area.

CULTURAL RESEARCH CENTER & ARIZONA CHRISTIAN UNIVERSITY

The Cultural Research Center (CRC) at Arizona Christian University was launched in August 2019 to conduct cutting-edge cultural and biblical worldview studies, providing credible research and resources to inform and mobilize strategic engagement in cultural transformation. The starting point of transforming culture is to get a clear picture of the worldviews that animate its landscape.

The goal of the Cultural Research Center is to become the nation's primary biblical worldview research hub. Arizona Christian University will continue to provide worldview education to college students, but that activity is just one of the many that relate to the core mission of Arizona Christian University—expanding the biblical worldview in America—both in the Church and in American culture.

As the biblical worldview research and resource arm of Arizona Christian University, the Cultural Research Center provides research and resources to individuals, families, churches, schools and universities, and organizations that seek to strategically increase the level of biblical worldview among people of faith and within American culture.

The Cultural Research Center also collaborates with other leading national organizations, with the goal of providing reliable research and effective resources for biblical worldview understanding within all areas of American culture.

The Cultural Research Center serves Arizona Christian University's worldview development efforts by measuring student worldview development using the Arizona Christian University Student Worldview Inventory (administered throughout each student's academic career). Arizona Christian University is committed to biblical worldview development and assessment in all facets of the student experience.

Arizona Christian University is one of the fastest-growing Christian universities in America and was recently ranked by *U.S. News & World Report* as the No. 1

Undergraduate Teaching Institution in the West. Arizona Christian University provides a biblically integrated, liberal arts education equipping graduates to serve the Lord Jesus Christ in all aspects of life as leaders of influence and excellence. Arizona Christian University exists to educate and equip followers of Christ to transform culture with truth

For more information about the Cultural Research Center, visit:
CulturalResearchCenter.com

For more information about Arizona Christian University, visit:
ArizonaChristian.edu

To access the Arizona Christian University Worldview Assessment, visit:
ACUWorldview.com

ARIZONA CHRISTIAN
UNIVERSITY

- America's premier biblical worldview university
- *US News & World Report* "Best College" seven years running
- 9th fastest-growing university in the nation
- Theologically and culturally conservative
- Degrees in seven areas of cultural influence
- Courageously Christian
- Educating leaders to "Transform Culture with Truth"

arizonachristian.edu

Cultural Research Center

culturalresearchcenter.com

Dr. George Barna
Director of Research

You can help change the world one conversation at a time.

It can be tough to know how to talk to other people about things that matter. So how can we all get better at building real relationships?

First, check out **JourneyCoaching.org**. You'll discover helpful-to-your-life podcasts, a simple-to-follow workbook, and relevant tools you'll need to start building the kind of relationships that can help make your life and the lives of others, well, just simply better.

Now that you've gone through *Journey toward Maximum Faith*, consider going through *Starting the Journey Personal Workbook* with a friend. It will help you explore in more depth your own life's story and how it fits in with God's bigger story, while building a trusting relationship.

The *Starting the Journey Personal Workbook* can help you bring a better version of yourself to the world, providing a pathway to more effectively "Go and make disciples."

And isn't that the ultimate life's work we're designed to do?

IF YOU WANT TO GROW, WE WANT TO HELP!

JOURNEYCOACHING.ORG